Activity Assemblies for Multi-racial Schools 5–11

Elizabeth Peirce

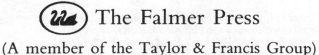 The Falmer Press

(A member of the Taylor & Francis Group)
London • Washington, DC

UK   The Falmer Press, 4 John Street, London WC1N 2ET

USA The Falmer Press, Taylor & Francis Inc., 1900 Frost Road, Suite 101, Bristol, PA 19007

First published in 1992

British Library Cataloguing in Publication Data

Peirce, Elizabeth
    Activity assemblies for multi-racial schools 5–11.
    I. Title
    372.84

    ISBN 0–75070–049–1

Jacket design by Caroline Archer

Typeset in 11/13 Bembo by
Graphicraft Typesetters Ltd, Hong Kong

Printed in Great Britain by Burgess Science Press, Basingstoke on paper which has a specified pH value on final paper manufacture of not less than 7·5 and is therefore 'acid free'.

Contents

Acknowledgements   viii

Introduction   1

1 New Beginnings   3
5–11   Who am I? (All)   4
5–9   The Creation Story (Judaism)   6
5–11   Chinese New Year: The Dance of the Years   12
5–11   Rosh Hashana and Yom Kippur (Judaism)   17
5–11   Vesākha: Buddhist New Year (Buddhism)   22
7–11   Baisakhi: Sikh New Year (Sikhism)   24

2 Places of Worship   27
5–11   Exploring a Synagogue (Judaism)   28
5–11   A visit to a Mosque (Islam)   36
7–11   Interview a Buddhist Monk (Buddhism)   39
7–11   A Gurdwara or House of God (Sikhism)   41

3 Friends   43
7–11   Jonathan and David (Judaism)   44
5–11   Muhammad Shows a way to remain Friends (Islam)   48
5–7   Making-Up (Indian Folk Story)   50
7–11   The First Brotherhood (Sikhism)   53

4 Clothes and Artefacts   57
5–11   Clothes we Wear (Sikhism)   58
5–11   Jewellery for a Hindu Bride (Hinduism)   60
5–11   Clothes (Islam)   61
7–11   A Robe for a Theravāda Buddhist Monk (Buddhism)   62

5 Festivals   65
7–11   Sukkot (Judaism)   66
5–11   Hannukah (Judaism)   69

Contents

5–11 Purim (Judaism)   72
5–11 Pesah (Judaism)   78
7–11 Kathina (Buddhism)   83
5–11 Diwali (Hinduism)   85
5–11 Diwali (Sikhism)   89
5–11 Navratri and Dussehra (Hinduism)   94
7–11 Ramadan and Eid–ul–Fitr (Islam)   96
5–11 Eid–ul–Adha (Islam)   97
5–7   Holi (Hinduism)   99
7–11 Hola Mohalla (Sikhism)   100

6   Rites of Passage   101
5–9   A Hindu Naming Ceremony (Hinduism)   102
5–11 Bar Mitzvah (Judaism)   103
5–7   A Sikh Wedding (Sikhism)   105
5–11 Buddha Teaches about Death (Buddhism)   107

7   Water Themes   111
5–11 Jonah (Judaism)   112
5–11 The Money Tree (Chinese Traditional Tale)   117
7–11 The Importance of Washing Before Prayers (Islam)   120
5–7   How the Kingfisher got it's Name (Indian Folk Story)   127

8   Animals and Birds   131
5–11 Daniel in the Lion's Den (Judaism)   132
5–7   The Boy who saved a Swan (Buddhism)   137
5–11 The Donkey in Lion's Clothing (Sikhism)   140
5–11 The Thirsty Dog (Islam)   144

9   Leaders   149
5–11 Abraham's Story (Judaism)   150
5–11 Muhammad (Peace be upon him) (Islam)   155
11   Mahatma Gandhi (Hinduism)   157
5–11 Siddhārtha Gautama (Buddhism)   161
5–11 Guru Nanak (Sikhism)   165

10   Some Further Background information for the   169
     Teachers' Reference (including pronunciation guides)
     Judaism   170
     Buddhism   183
     Hinduism   191
     Islam   202
     Sikhism   209

With Thanks

The author wishes to record her deepest gratitude and indebtedness to the following experts who kindly read and corrected the draft manuscript. Any content deficiences are the author's own. Each faith is so complex and interesting that it has been impossible to do justice to each group in a book of this size. Grateful thanks to Riadh el Droubie for reading the sections on Islam; Eleanor Nesbitt for reading the sections on Hinduism; Piara Singh Sambhi for reading the sections on Sikhism; Dr. Paul Williams for reading the sections on Buddhism; Angela Wood for reading the sections on Judaism and for suggesting the Jewish songs; Veronica Clark and Marjory Heasman for help with the music notation. The author would also like to record her thanks to the staff of the East Sussex Schools' Library Service (Eastbourne) for all their help.

Acknowledgements

'Peace is like gossamer' by Kate Compston, in *Leaves from the Tree of Peace*, published by The United Reformed Church, is reproduced with the kind permission of the author.

Sikh emblem and quotation, P. 106, in Collinson, C. and Miller, C. *Celebrations, Festivals in a Multi-Faith Community*, published by E. Arnold, 1985.

Line drawings based on photographs of tying a turban by Nick Hedges in Lyle, S. *Pavan is a Sikh*, A. and C. Black, 1977, reproduced with the kind permission of the publisher.

Adapted story 'The Money Tree' (E.C. Peirce) based on a story by Ken Ma, 'Beating the Tree', in *That'd be Telling* by M. Rosen and J. Griffiths, Cambridge University Press, 1985, is reproduced with the kind permission of Ken Ma.

Colour transparency by C. Fairclough of Rabbi and Barmitzvah boy, (p. 17), and black and white artwork of Hebrew script (p. 17), and inside of a synagogue (p. 15) both by Tony Payne, in Lawton, C. *My Belief — I am a Jew*, Franklin Watts, 1984, is reproduced with the kind permission of the publishers.

The Hindi script artwork by Tony Payne in Aggarwal, M. *My Belief — I am a Hindu*, (p. 17) Franklin Watts, 1984, is reproduced with the kind permission of the publishers.

Adapted story 'The Thirsty Dog' (E.C. Peirce) is based on a story told to the author by Riadh el Droubie entitled *A Thirsty Dog* and published by The Islamic Foundation, Leicester, 1990 in *Love All Creatures* by M.S. Kayani. The liberal adaptation here, is reproduced with the kind permission of the Islamic Foundation.

Adapted story, 'Making Up', (E.C. Peirce) is based on a story entitled *The Oldest and the Wisest* by T.C. Collocott in New Radiant Readers 5, published by Allied Publishers Limited, New Delhi, India.

Adapted story 'How the Kingfisher got it's name', (E.C. Peirce) is based on a story *How a Bird Got it's Lovely Colour* in Indian Folk Tales, published by Sabbash Publishers, Bombay, India.

The following illustrations are reproduced with the kind permission of Chansitor Publications Ltd., Norfolk.
1   The cycle of the chinese years, in *Chinese New Year* by A. Bancroft, published by R.M.E.P., 1984, p. 21.
2   The seder table in *Judaism in Words and Pictures*, by S. Thorley published by R.M.E.P., 1986, p. 23.
3   Outline of a mosque, in *Islam in Words and Pictures*, by S. Thorley, published by R.M.E.P., 1982, p. 9.

The illustrations and text, 'Ablutions before Prayer', and 'Prayer Positions', are reproduced with the kind permission of Minaret House, Croydon, Surrey.

Black and white transparencies of Ravan, Ganesh and Durga are reproduced with permission of Ann and Bury Peerless — Slide Resources and Picture Library.

Music notation for the following songs has been kindly arranged by Veronica Clark; Oz V' shalom, Der Rebbe, How Many Candles, Hodu l'Adonai Ki Tov. The songs were sung, taped, and translated by Angela Wood.

Tara Publications, N.Y. kindly gave permission to use the music notation for Hava Nagilah; lyrics by M. Nathanson and Yom ze M'chubad in Z'mirot Anthology.

ACUM, Israel, kindly gave permission for the following words and music; Ose Shalom, Ani Purim.

Naomi Shemer kindly gave permission to use the words and music of Be-Rosh Hashana from her book entitled the *The Second Book* published by 'Lulav' Israel Press Limited.

Psalm 150, 117, and most of the other biblical references are from the Good News Bible, published by Bible Society/Collins and are reproduced with the kind permission of the publishers. (Some references, where stated, are from the Revised Standardized Version of the Bible.)

Acknowledgements

Every effort has been made to trace the owners of all copyright material. In one or two cases this has proved impossible. The author will be pleased to correct any omissions in future editions and give full acknowledgements.

Introduction

In these times of great racial tension,* it is very important for all children to have some understanding of and insight into other people's religions. This is not a book which sets out to 'convert' children in state schools to other faiths, but rather an assembly book that attempts to 'inform' children about other people's beliefs.

Hence, children are introduced to the major places of worship; they are enabled to feel their way into other people's faiths, through the assemblies on Festivals; they are encouraged to see what it is like to stand in other people's shoes by looking at famous leaders; to learn some of the universal truths, through the teaching of the founders of the faiths, such as the Buddha's teaching about suffering and death etc. Kindness, wisdom, integrity honesty, truth, obedience etc. can be taught as well through Islam as through Judaism. It matters not so much which 'religious' order one belongs to, but how we treat one another in this multi-racial society. I am a Christian, but I need to understand what my Jewish or Muslim brethren think, what makes them tick, so that I can empathise with them and not condemn them, because of my stupid ignorance, just because they do not happen to believe what I believe. This, therefore, is my chief concern for all primary school children. If we learn about each others beliefs, we do not necessarily have to be disciples of them to understand them. Gandhi's achievements through non-violance, has lessons for us all.

It is the well rounded personality that is important; the need for children to learn love, mercy, justice, tolerance and truth in a variety of ways. Jesus said, 'Love your neighbour as yourself', perhaps this is the hardest concept of all, for all of mankind to learn.

I offer, what I hope is a child-centred approach to some of these deep, fundamental issues. This is the second volume in a two-part series. The first book is entitled *Activity Assemblies for Christian Collective Worship,*

* Written during the Gulf war 1991

which I hope will enable the non-specialist teacher to take broadly Christian assemblies in accordance with the 1988 Education Act. This book is intended to compliment the first book, by providing multi-faith assemblies. An attempt has been made to indicate the appropriate age-ranges for the assemblies and activities, but it must be understood, that these are only guidelines. The children's ability to understand and participate will vary enormously, according to many factors, including their intellectual and emotional readiness to grasp some of the ideas presented.

The teacher will be able to use many of the assemblies just as they are, other ideas will need considerable preparation and rehearsal before presentation to the whole school. Where possible, I have tried to indicate whether the piece offered, is an assembly or activity piece, or both.

Finally, in the text, I have tried to draw the teacher's attention to specific, important beliefs and practices in the introductory paragraphs of each assembly and also in the teachers' reference notes at the back of the book. (These are deliberately brief for easy/quick reference.) However, it is perhaps worth re-iterating some important points here. It should be noted that Muslims pay respect to Muhammad's name by saying the words 'Peace be upon him' each time his name is spoken. Also there is no music in Islamic services, therefore, I have not included hymns in the suggestions for Islamic assemblies; and although prayers have been suggested, the teacher must decide whether a time of quiet reflection is more appropriate for a particular assembly.

Jews, Christians and Muslims all see Abraham from different perspectives. These should be noted by the teacher and where there is a conflict of beliefs, these should be very carefully handled, with a clear explanation of the differences in belief. An example of this is in telling the story of Abraham and his willingness to sacrifice his son. Jews and Christians believe that it was Isaac who was prepared for sacrifice; Muslims believe that it was Ishma'ail.

Another area of difficulty between cultures may be the way each culture interprets the events of history. This will be as true for Hindus and Sikhs, as for Christians and Muslims. I have tried to be as fair as possible in my interpretation of events in the stories I have told.

If we are to draw all children together in an assembly, then some of these great stories from different world faiths must be retold. I have tried to do this, and in the telling, I have tried to bring the truth as it is seen from the point of view of the faith, indicated at the top of each assembly idea. All of us have something to learn from one another.

1   New Beginnings

5–11
Assembly
All

Who Am I?

At the beginning of the new school year, or a new term it is most important to remind the children about the sort of qualities that are needed in any community. With this in mind, think of the various qualities that you would like to encourage in school. Write down the words on large strips of card that can be, threaded with string and then worn around the neck of each child.

With careful preparation, the whole 5–11 age range can be involved in this assembly. The very youngest children can demonstrate, or explain, or paint their phrase e.g. 'I am helpful', whereas, an 11-year-old, could explain the meaning of 'I am a Peace-Maker', either by performing a short mime with one or two of his friends who are quarrelling, or by explaining other examples of peace-making activities.

This assembly has endless possibilities. Phrases such as the following could be included:

I am kind, I am helpful,
I am tolerant, I am polite,
I am caring, I am unselfish
I have patience, I can let others go before me,
I can be generous, I can let others have the best toy,
I can share, I can tell the truth,
I can comfort those in distress. etc.

At the end of the assembly, the class or group who has prepared the work can say together, 'I know who I am, who are you?'

Let the children meditate on this penetrating question, before closing with a simple prayer.

Prayer

Father God, make each one of us the sort of people you want us to be. Kind and helpful, caring and tolerant, ready to put others first. Amen.

Song

No. 35 'Take care of a friend' in *Every Colour Under the Sun*, published by Ward Lock Educational.

5–9
Assembly
Judaism

The Creation Story

A movement mime to involve the whole class or whole school.
You will need the following characters:
(Depending on the numbers of children, you wish to involve, you can add more children to each group).

> Children representing Darkness
> Children representing Light
> Children representing Earth
> Children representing Sea
> Children representing all kinds of Plants and Trees
> Child representing Sun
> Child representing Moon
> Children representing Stars
> Children representing all kinds of Creatures
> Children representing all kinds of Birds
> Children representing all kinds of Domestic Animals
> Children representing all kinds of Wild Animals
> Child representing first Man
> Child representing first Woman
> A Narrator

Simple costumes, headdresses and masks can be worn to enhance the characterization.

The story unfolds in the following way:

Narrator: This is the story about how God created the world. In the beginning there was nothing but darkness.

[Children dressed in black from head to foot, move about the hall spreading darkness. They come to rest in the front of the hall and build themselves in a black semi-circular structure, just touching at different points to represent night. See page 11 for music to which to dance.]

6

Narrator: And God said 'Let there be light and there was light'. (Good News Bible (GNB))

[Children dressed completely in white move about the hall, spreading light. They also come to rest opposite the children dressed in black at the front. Once again these children build themselves into a light semi-circular structure, just touching at different points to represent day.]

Narrator: (Pointing first to the white group of children, and then to the black group) 'God called the light Day, and the darkness he called Night. There was morning and evening on this first day.'

[The groups revolve around each other; the white group miming a lively 'waking-up' dance, and the black group miming a 'sleepy' dance. Both groups come together to form a morning and evening structure, before going back to sit in their places in the hall.]

Narrator: On the second day, God created the sky.

[Children dressed in blue, dotted all around the hall, stand up exactly where they are, and do a stretching, spreading dance, trying to reach their partners across the hall and then sit down.]

Narrator: And God said 'Let the waters under the heavens be gathered together into one place, and let the dry land appear'. And it was so. God called the dry land Earth, and the waters that were gathered together he called Seas. (Revised Standardized Version (RSV))

[Two groups; one dressed in brown representing the earth, and the other group dressed in different shades of green, representing the seas dance together. The whole scene can be made to look more effective if the 'sea' group dance with long strips of fabric which they pretend are the waves, and move in a wave-like dance across the 'earth' group.]

7

Narrator: And God created all kinds of plants and trees on this third day.

[Children wearing flower masks or twig headdress can do their dance.]

Narrator: And on the fourth day, God created the Sun, and the Moon and the Stars.

[A child dressed in a shift with a brilliant sun radiating outwards on both sides, can dance first. Similarly, a child with a crescent-shaped headdress, and a crescent-shaped moon collage attached to a shift, can do his/her dance. Finally, a number of children, representing the stars, with stars on their heads and silver cut-out stars, stitched onto simple shifts, can do their dance and then return to their places.]

Narrator: And on the fifth day, God created all the creatures that live in the sea and all the birds that fly in the air.

[Children dressed as all kinds of sea creatures have their turn to dance. Include an octopus and a whale as well as different types of fish. Children with bird masks can make flying movements around the hall.]

Narrator: And then God created all the creatures that live on the earth, creepy creatures, and crawlie creatures, wild animals and pets.

[A pageant of children march around the hall, showing off their different costumes to the rest of the children.]

Narrator: And God created the first man and woman and he blessed them and said they could rule over the animals and birds and fish and eat the fruits and plants. And this was the sixth day and God was very pleased with his work.

[Two children representing the first man and woman, can move across the hall looking at all the flowers and plants and animals.]

Narrator: On the seventh day, God looked at all his handiwork and saw that it was finished, so he rested. God blessed this seventh day and set it apart as a special day of rest.

End the assembly with a simple prayer of thanks to God for all his creatures and the beauty of the earth, the sea and the skies.

Hymn

No. 1 'Morning has broken', in *Come and Praise*, published by the BBC, or 'Yom ze M'chubad', in *Z'mirot Anthology*, Traditional Sabbath songs for the home. Compiled and edited by Neil Levin. Published by Tara Publications, Cedarhurst, N.Y. (see part 10 for pronunciation guide).

Yom zeh m'chubad mikol yamin, ki vo shabat tzur olamim.

Sheshet yamim taaseh m'lahteha, v'yom hashvii l'eloheha
Shabat lo taaseh vo m'laha, ki hol asa sheshet yamim.

Yom zeh ...

More than all other days the Sabbath is blessed;
for the Rock of all time made it His day of rest.

For completing your work He has given six days;
but the seventh belongs to your God.
On that day no work should be done,
for in six days He completed the work of creation.
    More than all other days the Sabbath is blessed;
    for the Rock of all time made it His day of rest.

ki vo sha - bat tzur o - la - mim tzur o - la - mim.

she - shet ya - mim ta - a - se m'lach-te - cha v' - yom ha-sh'-vi - i le - lo - he -cha

Sha - bat Sha - bat lo ta - a - se m'la - cha ki - chol a - sa - she-shet ya - mim.

Some Suggestions for Dance Music for The Creation Story

(Taken from the double cassette tape entitled Essential Classics; 33 of the Greatest Classics by Polygram Record Operations Ltd.)

Darkness	Massenet 'Thais' — Meditation. (Side 3 no. 2)
Light	Richard Strauss 'Also sprach Zarathustra' — Sunrise (Side 1 no. 1)
Sky	Rachmaninov Rhapsody on a theme of Paganini — Variation 18 (Side 3 no. 8)
Sea	Tchaikovsky 'The Nutcraker' — Waltz of the Flowers (Side 4 no. 4)
Earth	Falla 'El Amor brujo' — Ritual Fire Dance (Side 3 no. 9)
Plants, trees and Flowers	Mascagni 'Cavalleria Rusticana' — Intermezzo (Side 4 no. 2)
Sun, Moon, and Stars	Offenbach 'The Tales of Hoffman' — Barcarolle (Side 1 no. 7)
Sea Creatures and Birds	Grieg 'Peer Gynt' — Morning (Side 3 no. 4)
Creepy Crawlies	Wagner 'Ride of the Valkyries' (Side 3 no. 3)
Man and woman	Pachelbel Canon and Gigue (Side 3 no. 6)

**5–11
Assembly
All**

Chinese New Year: The Dance of the Years

The diagram is taken from 'Chinese New Year', the Living Festival Series, by Anne Bancroft, published by Religious and Moral Education Press, Exeter 1984, page 21. Reproduced by kind permission of Chansitor Publications Ltd.

The Chinese New Year follows the lunar calendar. It usually takes place in January or February depending when the second new moon occurs, after the winter solstice. The actual celebrations for the new year can last for fifteen nights, with each night having a special significance and festival. For instance, the eighth night is called 'The Night of the Stars'. Little oil lights are lit and hung around the house to keep away evil spirits. The thirteenth night is part of the Lantern Festival, when everyone carries beautiful, different shaped and coloured lanterns in the street. Perhaps the most famous night of all, is the last night, the night of the Dragon Dance.

Any of these festivals provide suitable material for activity assemblies to perform for the rest of the school in music, movement and dance. For this assembly, it will be assumed that a **dance for the years** has been chosen for younger children. Simple masks and costumes will be needed, for the following named years:

> The year of the Tiger
> The year of the Rabbit
> The year of the Dragon
> The year of the Snake
> The year of the Horse
> The year of the Sheep
> The year of the Monkey
> The year of the Cockerel
> The year of the Dog
> The year of the Pig
> The year of the Rat
> The year of the Buffalo
> Narrator

For the second part of the assembly, older children could choose a significant *event* which happened during each one of the above cycles i.e. the outbreak of World War 2 in 1939, in the Year of the Rabbit, or the Olympic Games in 1988, the Year of the Dragon. Then each of the years will have a partner, who will mime the special event.

Suggestions for the events could be as follows (although teachers may prefer to think of their own):

The Tiger	1914 Outbreak of the First World War
The Rabbit	1987 The Great Storm in Britain
The Dragon	1988 the Seoul Olympic Games
The Snake	1989 the demolition of the Berlin Wall
The Horse	1966 the 900th Anniversary of the Norman Conquest of England
The Sheep	1919 First direct flight across the Atlantic by Alcock and Brown
The Monkey	1992 Single European Market
The Cockerel	1945 End of the Second World War
The Dog	1922 Treasure found in Tutankhamun's tomb
The Pig	1947 School leaving age raised to 15 years in Great Britain
The Rat	1936 Accession and Abdication of King Edward VIII
The Buffalo	1961 Gagarin made the first space flight

The dance takes place in the round. All the main characters sit in a circle, with the rest of the assembled children and parents (if it is to be a parents' assembly) sitting around and behind the main dancers.

The Narrator needs to explain that the children will dance the different *animal* signs for each Chinese year and that the legend behind the naming of the years is supposed to come from the fact that twelve creatures came to say farewell to the Buddha, when he was leaving this planet, therefore he named each year after each of the following dancing animals.

Some explanation also needs to be given, about the fact that it is a twelve-year cycle, and that the cycle keeps repeating itself, so that the Tiger always follows the Buffalo etc.

If it is decided that more than one class is to be involved in the dance, then the Narrator can introduce each section in the following way: 'These are the tiger years, 1914, 1926, 1938, 1950, 1974, 1986. The tigers will now dance for you.' Suitable taped music is played, as the tigers dance their dance. Labels can be pinned to the costumes, to denote the year that the child is representing. (See pages 15–16 for suggestions for dance music)

In addition to the simple costumes, masks, leotards and tights; the rabbits could also wear powder puffs, the cockerels could wear plumes or combs, the rats could wear tails, the horses could wear manes or ride on simple hobby horses made out of a dowling stick and a horse's head, consisting of some tights stuffed with newspaper (see picture below).

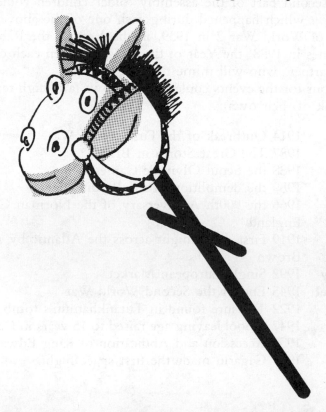

For the dragon dance, as well as the taped music, percussion instruments could be played, such as the cymbals. Percussion instruments could also enhance the music of the other dances, such as the rats or monkeys.

A ribbon attached to a dowling rod makes a very pretty alternative to the character dancing. For instance the snakes could simply stand in the centre of the circle and wave their rods and ribbons to snake-like music.

For the second part of the assembly, the Narrator needs to introduce the pairs of significant *dates* with their partner i.e. 'This is 1914 in the year of the Tiger, the outbreak of World War I'; 'This is 1987 in the year of the rabbit, the year of the Great Storm in Britain' etc. The pairs of children can then process and mime their parts around the circle, wearing their simple costumes and labels denoting the event, before returning to their seats.

End the assembly with the actual year, and a forceful message for the New Year i.e. 'This is 1996, the year when we must feed the starving people in the world'.

Prayer

Heavenly Father, make us conscious, this New Year, of the needs of others. Help us to give generously, of our time, and talents, and money to help others. Amen.

Hymn

No. 141 'Tomorrow is a highway broad and fair,' in *New Life*, published by Galliard; or No. 106, 'It's a new day, there's hope,' in *Come and Praise 2*, published by the BBC, London, 1988.

Some Suggestions for Dance Music for the Dance of the Years

(Taken from four cassettes entitled 'Classics by Candlelight' by Stylus Music Ltd.)

Tigers   Strauss Roses from the South Waltz (vol 4; side 2; no. 5)
Rabbits   Strauss Pizzicato Polka (vol 4; side 2; no. 6)
Dragon   Gounod Ballet Music from Faust no. 2 Extract (vol 2; side 2; no. 6)
Snake   Schubert Impromptu no. 4 in A Flat (vol 4; side 1; no. 4)
Horses   Tchaikovsky Waltz from Sleeping Beauty (vol 4; side 2; no. 7)

Sheep   Mozart Andante from Piano Concerto no. 21 (vol 4; side 1; no. 1)

Monkey   Tchaikovsky Dance of the Sugar Plum Fairy from the Nut-cracker Suite (vol 4; side 2; no. 8)

Cockerel   Mozart Romanze from 'Eine Kleine Nachtmusik' (vol 4; side 1; no. 2)

Dog   Mendelssohn 'Spring Song' Song without Words Op 62 no. 6 (vol 3; side 2; no. 9)

Pig   Schubert Andantino from 'Rosamunde' (vol 4; side 1; no. 3)

Rat   Haydn Minuet and Trio from Symphony no. 83 'La Poule' (vol 3; side 1; no. 5)

Buffalo   Gounod Ballet Music from Faust no. 1 Extract (vol 2; side 2; no. 7)

(It should be noted that modern popular music can be used just as effectively as classical music).

Rosh Hashana and Yom Kippur

Rosh Hashana, the Jewish New Year, takes place in the Hebrew month of Tishri, that is September or October.

Try to find a picture of a Shofar or ram's horn to show the children, or visit the Jewish Museum in London and see a real one (see address on page 29). A shofar is blown in the synagogue at this time. Jews send each other New Year cards, and eat apples or hallah (bread) which has been dipped in honey. This symbolizes the Jewish wish for a happy and sweet New Year.

It is also a time to make a fresh start and to ask God's forgiveness for sins. The Day of Atonement, that follows ten days after Rosh Hashana, is called Yom Kippur. During these ten days, Jews say sorry to their friends and neighbours for anything they may have done to hurt each other. They try to make amends for all wrong doings and ask God's forgiveness too. Of course, they do this at other times of the year, but this is the special festival for new beginnings.

At Rosh Hashana families go to the synagogue for a special service. Someone is chosen to read from the Sacred Scrolls, Psalms are sung and a sermon is preached, prayers are said. The distinctive part of the service is the blowing of the ram's horn. Sometimes, Jews go to the sea-side or to rivers, and empty their pockets and throw away any crumbs on to the water. This is called Tashlich or throwing away. It is a symbol of throwing away old sins, bad thoughts and deeds.

Families enjoy special Rosh Hashana meals together. Bread is baked in different shapes i.e. Ladders 'as a symbol of prayers rising to God', or Crowns 'because God, the Creator, is King of the world' (From: *A Jewish Family in Britain* by Vida Barnett, Published by R.M.E.P.).
Then after the fast of Yom Kippur, Jews believe God will forgive their sins and seal their names in the 'Book of Life' (Barnett).

Why not teach your class one of the shorter Psalms, like Psalm 150. This could be done as a choral speaking exercise. The words could be softly spoken in the beginning and then built up to a crescendo. (See Psalm 150 below, taken from the Good News Bible, published by Bible Society/Collins.)

During the assembly, ask the children to think of any bad things in their minds that they could metaphorically throw away, something bad that they have done or thought and will try not to do again.

Make a display of the instruments mentioned in Psalm 150 i.e. drums, flutes, cymbals etc. These could be played at the appropriate times either before the choral speaking or during the piece, or afterwards.

PSALM 150

1 Praise the Lord!
  Praise God in his Temple!
  Praise his strength in heaven!
2 Praise him for the mighty things he has done.
  Praise his supreme greatness.
3 Praise him with trumpets.
  Praise him with harps and lyres.
4 Praise him with drums and dancing.
  Praise him with harps and flutes.
5 Praise him with cymbals.
  Praise him with loud cymbals.
6 Praise the LORD, all living creatures!
  Praise the LORD!

End with a simple prayer asking god's forgiveness for all wrong deeds.

Prayer

O Father God, we ask your forgiveness for all the wrong thoughts and words and deeds that we have committed. Help us to make a fresh start today and to live our lives in love and peace and harmony with each other. Amen.

Song

'On New Year'/Be-Rosh Hashana is a modern song written by a popular Israeli vocalist and composer called Naomi Shemer. It is about the Jewish New Year but fits any time of fresh starts and new beginnings. (A.W.) (see Part 10 for pronunciation guide).

On New Year/Be-Rosh Hashana from 'Naomi Shemer,
The Second Book, published by 'Lulav' Israel Press Limited

Be-rosh hashana, be-rosh hashana
Parcha shoshana etzli ba gina
Be-rosh hashana sira levana
Agena la bachof pitom

Be-rosh hashana, be-rosh hashana
Libbenu ana bitfilla noshana
Sheyafa ve shona tehe ha shana
Asher matchila ha yom.

La la la la la la
Yafa veshona tehe ha shana
Asher matchila ha yom.

Be-rosh hashana be-rosh hashana
Parcha anana birkia ha setav
Be-rosh hashana kener neshama
Ala ba sade hatzav

Be-rosh hashana be-rosh hashana
Libbenu ana bitfilla noshana
Sheyafa veshona tehe ha shana
Asher matchila la akhshav.

La la la la la la
Yafa veshona tehe ha shana
Asher matchila la akhshav

Be-rosh hashana, be-rosh hashana
Parcha mangina she'ish lo hikkir
Vetokh yemama ha zemer hama
Mikkol hallonot ha ir.

Be-rosh hashana be-rosh hashana
Libbenu ana bitfilla noshana
Sheyafa veshona tehe ha shana
Asher matchila la akhshav.

La la la la la la
Yafa veshona tehe ha shana
Asher matchila la akhshav.

On new year's eve
A rose bloomed in my garden,
A white boat
Anchored suddenly in my shore.

On new year's eve,
Our heart answered with an old prayer,

La la la la la la
For a better and different year
Starting today.

On new year's eve
Rode a cloud in the autumn skies,
In the field, like a candle
Grew the squill.

On new year's eve
Our heart answered with an old prayer,
For a better and different year
That's starting now.

La la la la la la
For a better and different year
Starting today.

On new year's eve
A melody was born, which no one knew,
And within a day a song was heard
Throughout the town.

On new year's eve
Our hearts answered with an old prayer
For a better and different year
Starting now.

La la la la la la
For a better and different year
Starting today.

Be - rosh ha - sha - na be - rosh ha - sha - na par - cha sho - sha - na ets - li ba - gi - na be - rosh ha - sha - na si - ra le - va - na ag - na la ba - chof pi - tom be - rosh ha - sha - na be - rosh ha - sha - na li - be - nu a - na bit - fi - la no - sha - na she - ya fa ve - sho - na te - he ha - sha - na a - sher mat - chi - la la ha - yom la yom.

5–11
Activity/Assembly
Buddhism

Vesākha or the Buddhist New Year

This is the most important full moon festival for Theravāda Buddhists. (See Part 10 for note about Theravāda Buddhism.) It is usually held in April or May. It is the celebration of the Buddha's birth, his Enlightenment and his death.

As a New Year celebration, it could be a time when children could remember some of the teachings of the Buddha i.e. not to harm animals, not to steal, not to tell lies etc. (See part 10 for further information.)

Perhaps one of the Jātaka stories could be retold (see 'Twenty Jātaka Tales' by N.I. Khan published by London and The Hague, East-West Publications).

It is also known as the Festival of Lights, because candles are lit, standing for Enlightment and incense is burnt. Buddhists visit the temple on this day and give of money to the poor. Since the Buddha taught his followers that they should hurt no living thing, perhaps the school could use this occasion to support a charity for the Protection of Animals (i.e. RSPCA, RSPB see addresses below). Generous giving, is part of the Buddhist tradition at Vesākha.

In addition, because the lotus flower has become a symbol of the Buddha's Enlightenment, perhaps the children could make a large frieze of lotus flowers, for this New Year assembly, and make individual lotus badges as a sign that they will try to be kind to animals and to one another.

'The lotus is a symbol of enlightenment since it grows in muddy water (samsara) but raises it's flower on a long stem to the sun (enlightenment)'. (*World Religions in Education Festivals*. The Shap Working Party on World Religions in Education, published by Commission for Racial Equality, London 1987, page 20.) Lotus flowers can be made out of crêpe paper using the pear shapes opposite.

Prayer

Almighty God, who made the world and all the creatures in it, help us today, to be kind to all animals and to each other and to give generously to those societies who work for the protection of animals. Amen.

Hymn

No. 80 'All the animals that I have ever seen', in *Come and Praise 2*, published by the BBC, London, 1988.

Addresses:
Royal Society for the Prevention of Cruelty to Animals
The Manor House
The Causeway
Horsham
West Sussex RH12 1HG
Telephone No. 0403 64181

Royal Society for the Protection of Birds
The Lodge
Sandy
Bedfordshire SG19 2DL
Telephone No. 0767 680551

7–11
Activity/Assembly
Sikhism

Baisakhi: Sikh New Year

For Sikhs, this is the most important festival. It commemorates the formation of the Khalsa or first Sikh brotherhood of arms in 1699, by the tenth
and last human Guru, Guru Gobind Singh. (See page 53 for the festival
drama).

It also commemorates the beginning of the Sikh New Year and is
accompanied by an elaborate celebration and a continuous reading of the
Guru Granth Sahib, the Sikh's Holy book. It was originally a Hindu
Festival but the third Sikh Guru, Guru Amar Das, in the middle of the 16th
century commanded his followers to meet on this day, for their own
festival to show Sikh solidarity and unity.

Today, the festival takes place on the 13th or 14th of April and if this
falls on a weekday, the Guru Granth Sahib will be read continuously, for
forty-eight hours before the main celebration which is usually held on the
nearest Sunday. The reading is completed on the morning of the celebration.
This continuous reading from the holy book is known as Akhand Path,
(page 108, *Celebrations: Festivals in a Multi-Faith Community* by C. Collinson
and C. Miller, published by Edward Arnold, London, 1985).

Prayers are said, and Karah Prasad, the Sikh's holy food, is distributed
to each person in the Gurdwara. An important part of the festival is the
renewal of the Sikh flag, called the Nishan Sahib. There is always a flag and
a flagpole outside a Sikh Gurdwara to denote that it is a place of worship.

Once the ceremony is in progress, the flagpole is lowered and the old
flag, and flagpole coverings are removed. The flagpole is then carefully
washed and many of the worshippers will bow before the pole as a mark of
respect. It is recovered with fabric and a new flag is inserted. Five men,
representing the five men who were prepared to die for their Guru (see
pages 53–55) will bless the flag and lead the worshippers back into the Gurdwara for the festival meal. The meal is prepared by the women and usually
consists of a vegetable curry and rice, and chapatis, a special kind of bread.

Often during the Baisakhi Festival, the Amrit Sanskar ceremony will
take place (see page 213). This is the ceremony where Sikh men and
women commit themselves to the Sikh faith and to the Khalsa (brotherhood).

Before the communal meal, hymns from the Guru Granth Sahib are
sung and a lecture is given to the people, reminding them of the important

aspects of being a Sikh. The ceremony ends with everyone wishing each other a happy new year.

The emblem on the flag is a picture of the double-edged sword or Khanda. 'One edge symbolizes God's power and justice, the other freedom and authority given to the man who obeys God. On the outside of the Khanda, in the emblem, are two curved swords symbolizing religious and political freedom; it was for this cause that Guru Gobind Singh founded the Khalsa. Surrounding the Khanda is the Chackra, a circle symbolic of the unity of the Sikhs and their belief in one God "whose name is truth".' (C. Collinson and C. Miller, p. 109)

Source: *Celebrations: Festivals in a Multi-faith Community,* by C. Collinson and C. Miller, Edward Arnold, 1985, p. 106.

For this assembly talk about the symbolism portrayed on the flag and ask the children to design their own flags which could embody the ideals of the school community or a friendship club. The children could work in groups of three to produce their own flag. The teacher may need to suggest topics for symbolism, e.g. honesty, but the children will have many ideas of their own including the symbols for clubs that they may have already joined.

End the assembly with a parade of flags and a brief explanation of the word/s that are being depicted.

Prayer

Father God, today we have been reminded of truth, justice, freedom, unity and peace. May these qualities abound in our school. Amen.

Hymn

No. 37 'Working Together', in *Every Colour Under the Sun*' published by Ward Lock Educational.

2   Places of Worship

5–11
Activity
Judaism

Exploring a Synagogue

In Britain today, there are many synagogues. Before involving the children in a class project, the teacher will need to make a preparatory visit, in order to establish whether the local synagogue is an Orthodox one, or whether it is one of the Reform or Progressive synagogues. There will be some differences in styles of worship etc.

It is also important to know something about the layout of the synagogue, the architecture, furniture, history etc. and the provision of toilets.

Perhaps the local Rabbi could be invited into a school assembly prior to the visit, to talk about special features that can be seen inside and outside the synagogue, or slides could be shown. It is important that the teacher, briefs the Rabbi, beforehand. For instance, he will need to know the age range of the children, the sort of language levels; something about the child-centred approach; permission to tell funny stories.

It is important to decide how the project work is to be tackled; individual work, small groups or the whole class. Very young children may find it simpler to work in small groups with a parent helper, concentrating on one particular aspect of the synagogue. Then the whole class could come together at the end of the project to share their findings. Older children may like to have a prepared work-sheet of items to look out for and then to concentrate on and to research one particular aspect of the synagogue that interests them — or make their own project book about the artefacts.

Approximately half an hour should be allowed for the visit for the younger children. Older children may need a little longer.

Prepare the children by asking them to stand quite still inside the synagogue and listen to the sounds in the building. Remind the children not to shout or run about, but to treat the place with respect.

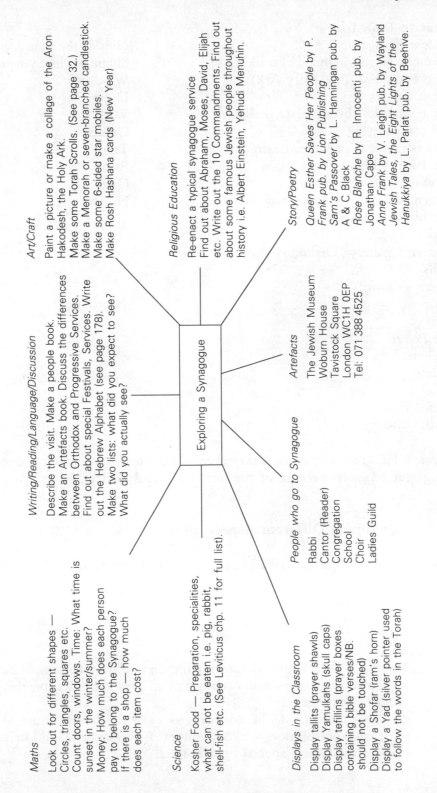

Art/Craft

Paint a picture or make a collage of the Aron Hakodesh, the Holy Ark.
Make some Torah Scrolls. (See page 32.)
Make a Menorah or seven-branched candlestick.
Make some 6-sided star mobiles.
Make Rosh Hashana cards (New Year)

Religious Education

Re-enact a typical synagogue service
Find out about Abraham, Moses, David, Elijah etc. Write out the 10 Commandments. Find out about some famous Jewish people throughout history i.e. Albert Einstein, Yehudi Menuhin.

Story/Poetry

Queen Esther Saves Her People by P. Frank pub. by Lion Publishing
Sam's Passover by L. Hanningan pub. by A & C Black
Rose Blanche by R. Innocenti pub. by Jonathan Cape
Anne Frank by V. Leigh pub. by Wayland
Jewish Tales, the Eight Lights of the Hanukkiya by L. Parlat pub. by Beehive.

Writing/Reading/Language/Discussion

Describe the visit. Make a people book.
Make an Artefacts book. Discuss the differences between Orthodox and Progressive Services.
Find out about special Festivals, Services. Write out the Hebrew Alphabet (see page 178).
Make two lists: what did you expect to see?
What did you actually see?

Exploring a Synagogue

Artefacts

The Jewish Museum
Woburn House
Tavistock Square
London WC1H 0EP
Tel: 071 388 4525

Maths

Look out for different shapes — Circles, triangles, squares etc.
Count doors, windows. Time: What time is sunset in the winter/summer?
Money: How much does each person pay to belong to the Synagogue?
If there is a shop — how much does each item cost?

Science

Kosher Food — Preparation, specialities, what can not be eaten i.e. pig, rabbit, shell-fish etc. (See Leviticus chp. 11 for full list).

People who go to Synagogue

Rabbi
Cantor (Reader)
Congregation
School
Choir
Ladies Guild

Displays in the Classroom

Display tallits (prayer shawls)
Display Yamulkahs (skull caps)
Display tefillins (prayer boxes containing bible verses/NB. should not be touched)
Display a Shofar (ram's horn)
Display a Yad (silver pointer used to follow the words in the Torah)

What to look for

Inside a Synagogue	*Outside the Synagogue*
Menorah (seven-branched candlestick)	Shape of the Synagogue
Aron Hakodesh (the Holy Ark)	Windows
Torah Scrolls	Doors
Torah Mantles, breast plate, bells	Walls
Yad (or pointer)	Garden
Tablets of the Ten Commandments	Trees
The lamp which is kept alight	Roof
showing God's presence	Gates
Magen David (6-pointed star)	Notices
The bimah (raised platform)	
Seats	
Women's gallery (Orthodox Jews)	
Walls	
Décor — motifs	
Floor	
Roof	
The Foyer	
Kitchen	
Toilets	
Office	
School Room	
Rabbi's Study	

Question: Find out why there is no graveyard or tombstones attached to the synagogue (*Answer*: because of the need for ritual purity).

Developing Different Aspects of the Work

(A few aspects will be described in more detail. Refer to flow diagram for other aspects).

Writing

1   Make a People book. Younger children could make simple books with just one sentence on each page i.e. This is the Rabbi, this is a Bar Mitzvah boy etc.
     Older children could be encouraged to write a little more about what each person does i.e. A member of the Ladies Guild helps to prepare food for a special occasion etc.

Rabbi and Bar Mitzvah Boy

Source: *My Belief: I am a Jew,* by C. Lawton published by Franklin Watts, 1984 (photograph by Chris Fairclough)

2 A large class book could be made containing pictures and writing about the artefacts found in the synagogue i.e. Tallits, yamulkahs, Torah Scrolls etc.

3 Older children could write out the Ten Commandments and decorate the borders. (N.B. no living creatures.)

4 Make a concertina book, showing the sequence of Shabbat. (Sabbath, see pages 33–35)

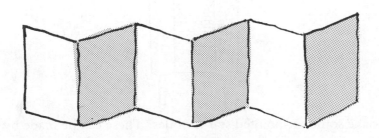

Mathematics

1 Look for different shapes; circles, triangles, squares in the building etc. Look out for symmetry in the synagogue.
2 Count the doors, windows, seats etc.
3 Try to obtain a timetable for sunset times during summer and winter months, so that Sabbath Eve Services (Orthodox Jews) can be worked out. (see pages 33–35) Make a chart so that comparisons can be made.
4 Money. How much does each person pay to belong to the synagogue? How is the money used?
   Is there a synagogue shop? What sort of items are sold and how much do things cost?

Art/Craft

1 Make a large fabric collage of the Aron Hakodesh, the Holy Ark, with the 'dressed' Torah Scrolls inside.

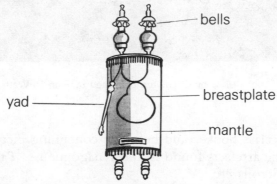

2 Let the children make individual replicas of the Torah Scrolls using a roll of paper and two dowling rods. (See also p. 31).

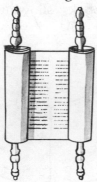

3 Make some six-pointed star mobiles. These can be made by joining two triangles together to make a star shape. Make large and small

stars for effect, and suspend them from hoops hanging from the ceiling. Stars could be decorated with silver paper, silver paint or crayon.

4   Make some Rosh Hashana (New Year) cards.
Pictures of Israel (obtainable from Travel brochures) could be cut out and stuck onto cards, or children could design their own card by using the star motif or special shofar motif or other artefacts found in synagogues today. If the latter method is chosen, perhaps the children could print their own cards using potato/lino prints.

R E/Assembly

This could take the form of re-enacting a typical Sabbath Service. It must be decided whether the service is to be strictly Orthodox in character, or like one of the Reform services. For this purpose, an Orthodox service will be described.

The Sabbath evening service begins fifteen minutes before sunset (see time-table). The Sabbath morning service will commence around nine o'clock the next day and will last for approximately two or three hours.

Men and women are segregated. The men sit in the main part of the synagogue, whilst the women sit in the women's gallery. Men and married women must cover their heads, and men put on their special prayer shawls to pray.

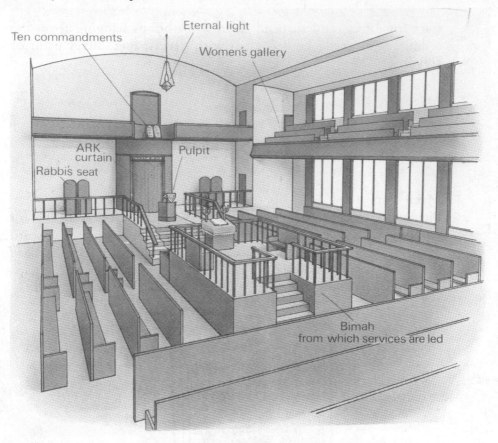

Source: *My Belief: I am a Jew*, C. Lawton, Franklin Watts, 1984 Artwork by Tony Payne.
Reproduced by kind permission of Franklin Watts.

The service is in Hebrew and the most important part of the service is when the Torah is read. A Torah scroll is taken out of the Ark, and after some prayers have been said, it is taken around the synagogue. Some people bow before the scroll as a mark of respect. Seven men usually have the honour of being called up to the bimah or platform to read from the Torah. Then it is held up for everyone to see the words. A yad, or pointer is used for reading the scroll, as the words are Holy and must not be touched. After the reading, the scroll is dressed before it is returned to the ark. It is dressed with a special mantle, breastplate, yad and bells.

There are also readings from the Haftara or Prophets which are also in Hebrew. Then prayers are said before the sermon. The Rabbi preaches the sermon and will display his great learning by explaining the scriptures.

After the service, the congregation often joins together for the blessing or kiddush. This is said over wine and challot, the special twisted loaves of bread. Everyone can have a piece of bread and drink some of the wine, although children usually drink orange juice.

The rest of the day, of course, is spent at rest, as God commanded. No work is done, the meals have been prepared and cooked the day before and so the family spend the day relaxing together.

End the assembly with a short prayer of thanks to God for his Holy words and the day of rest.

Hymn

'The Sabbath Day', in *Shalom, Songs for Children in the Jewish tradition*, translated and explained by A. Baron. (Address for words and music is on page 177).

5–11
Activity/Assembly
Islam

A Visit to a Mosque

For this assembly you will need a large line drawing or poster of the inside/outside of a mosque. (see page 38) If there is a mosque in your town, of course it would be preferrable to make a visit, working along similar cross-curricular lines to those outlined on pages 28–35 (exploring a Synagogue). Perhaps the class could visit the Central London Mosque in Regent's Park (Tel: 071–724–3343 for an appointment.) Prepare a list of questions to ask, and look out for special features, based on the information given below.

Pin the poster to an easil. You will also need some large labels with the following words:

Outside

Dome	architectural feature to denote that the building is a mosque.
Minarets	vertical towers with small domes at the top. In Islamic countries, worshippers are called to prayer by the prayer-caller, from the top of the Minaret. Muslims everywhere are called to prayer five times a day.
Muezzin	the prayer-caller.
Fountain or Pool	In Islamic countries this is provided for washing before prayers, and for drinking.
Islamic arches	these can be seen above the windows and doors or in the courtyards surrounding the mosques. See picture below.

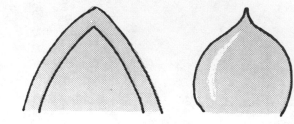
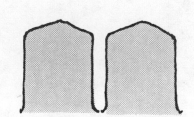

Patterns   beautiful geometric designs and Arabic Script can often be seen as decorations on the Minarets and walls.

Inside
No pictures, no seats, no statues, no music, no singing; shoes must be removed.

Shoe-rack   everyone takes off his or her shoes before entering the mosque

Washroom   ritual washing always precedes prayers. In some mosques there is a separate washroom for women. (See washing procedure on pages 122–123)

6 Clocks   the times when Muslims should pray are displayed on the clocks. A Muslim prays five times a day so the clocks denote the appropriate times. Of course, prayer times vary in winter and summer months as sunset/sunrise varies. The sixth clock shows the time of the main Friday prayers.

Mihrab   an alcove in the mosque showing the direction of Makkah.

Minbar   the flight of steps from the top of which the Imam speaks to the people.

Prayer mats   beautiful mats or rugs on which to pray.

Prayer hats   most Muslims always cover their heads when they pray

Agarbattis   incense sticks usually burned during Friday worship

The Qur'an   this is the Muslim's Holy Book.

Wooden stand   the Qur'an is raised above the floor and placed on a simple wooden stand.

Imam   this is a prayer leader

Women   generally women worship at home, although young girls in Britain, before the age of twelve, will come to the mosque to participate in Islamic classes. There is a special part of the mosque, away from the men, where women may pray.

Mosque classes   in some mosques in Britain, children attend mosque classes, between the ages of 5–12 years, on five nights a week, from about five o'clock until eight o'clock. Islamic studies are taught in the Pakistani language of Urdu. Arabic is also taught because the Qur'an is written in Arabic. Stories about the life of Muhammad are also studied.

Using the large picture of the mosque and the words on cards, the teacher takes each word in turn, and after giving a brief explanation, fixes the word in the appropriate position on the poster. When the picture has been completed, the teacher can talk about the wonderful Islamic designs and ask the children, if they know how to tell a real Persian carpet from a fake one. Briefly, it is this; in a genuine Persian carpet, there is always a tiny deliberate mistake, because Muslims believe that only God can create perfection. Therefore, a tiny flaw, reminds the carpet-makers of their in-equality with God.

Let the children experiment with geometric designs, and show the work that they have produced as a result of their research.

Prayer

God, we know that only you are perfect. Forgive our imperfections. Amen.

Outline of a Mosque

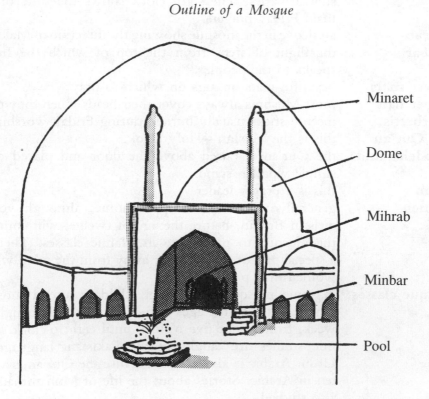

Minaret

Dome

Mihrab

Minbar

Pool

Source: *Islam in Words and Pictures*, S. Thorley, REMP, 1982. Reproduced by kind permission of Chansitor Publications Ltd.

Interview a Buddhist Monk or Nun

Invite a local monk or nun into school, to tell the children about his/her life, work, and the monastery where he/she lives. This assembly could be extended to leaders of other faiths. However, it is important to prepare the children first, by thinking out some interview questions, that they might like to ask their visitor, during the assembly. The teacher should ascertain whether the monk or nun follows the Theravāda tradition, or the Tibetan tradition, before asking the following questions. For instance, it is appropriate to ask a Tibetan monk about prayer flags, but not a Theravāda monk, and it is appropriate to ask a Theravāda monk about the number of meals per day, but not a Tibetan monk. (See page 185 for further information.)

1 Why did you choose to become a monk? Is there a special ceremony? What age do you have to be?
2 What rules do you live by? (See the basic precepts of a monk or nun on pages 39–40 and pages 185–186.)
3 Describe a typical day at the monastery.
4 Why do you wear a special robe? (See also pages 62–63).
5 How many meals do you eat a day? What kind of food do you eat? (Theravāda monk).
6 What is meditation?
7 What are Mantras? (Prayers). What do you say? Do you use prayer beads to help you pray? How many prayer beads are there? What do you write on prayer flags? (Tibetan monk).
8 Do children come to the monastery?
9 Do you have services?
10 Do you have a special day of worship?

It would be a nice idea if the children could bake a special dish or make a special salad that could be given to the monk at the end of his visit, to be taken back and shared with his fellow monks.

These are the basic precepts of a monk or nun. (They also apply to novices).

1 Not to destroy or harm life
2 Not to steal

3 Not to commit adultery or to have irresponsible sexual relations
4 Not to tell lies
5 Not to take intoxicating drinks or to take drugs
6 Not to eat other than at meal-times
7 Not to go entertainments like shows, with dancing or music
-8 Not to wear perfumes or scents or wear ornaments and decoration
9 Not to sleep on comfortable raised beds
10 Not to accept or handle gold or silver

(From: pages 33–34 *Buddhists and Buddhism* by M. Patrick, published by Wayland, East Sussex, 1982).

End the assembly with a short prayer of thanks to God for the visitor, and for all that has been learnt.

Prayer

Thank you God, for all that we have learnt today. May we always be ready to give generously to those in need. Amen.

Hymn

No. 18 'My mind to me a kingdom is', in *Every Colour Under the Sun*, published by Ward Lock Educational.

A Gurdwara or House of God

Try to arrange a visit to a Gurdwara, or House of God, but remember, shoes must be removed and heads must be covered.
What to look for inside the Gurdwara:

The Guru Granth Sahib	the Sikh's Holy book.
Palki	a sort of throne on which the Guru Granth Sahib is placed.
Cushions	the Holy book rests on beautifully decorated cushions in the Palki.
Offerings	money or food is placed in front of the Guru Granth Sahib by each member of the congregation.
Seating arrangements	everyone sits on the floor. Men usually sit on one side of the Gurdwara, women sit on the other side.
Karah Prasad	the Sikh's holy food is distributed to all the members of the congregation at the end of a service.
Kitchen	a very important room in the Gurdwara, as a communal meal called langar is prepared in the kitchen and offered to all worshippers after the service.

Make a list of questions to ask the Granthi or reader. (There are no priests or ministers).

1 Which day is the day of worship? (In Britain, it tends to be Sunday).
2 In what language is the service conducted? (Usually Punjabi, but sometimes parts of the service may be conducted in English in this country).
3 How long does a service last? (Usually three or four hours but worshippers are free to come and go as they please).
4 Are hymns sung? (Hymns from the Guru Granth Sahib, called Shabads are sung).

5   Are musical instruments used in worship? (Often a harmonium and pair of small drums are used).

6   What does the reader do? (The reader reads short passages from the Guru Granth Sahib and may give an explanation of the reading).

7   What sort of training would a Granthi need? (He will have a great knowledge of the Holy book and be able to teach others).

8   What provision is there for children? (There are Sunday Schools for children in Britain. Children are taught verses from the Guru Granth Sahib and will also learn the Gurmukhi script).

9   Are there special services for initiation, weddings and funerals? (See pages 105 and 210–211).

10 What other meetings take place during the week? (Some Gurdwaras hold special meetings for young people and community meetings).

Gather all the information together and finally let one group of children draw a ground floor plan of the inside of the Gurdwara and another group draw the outside of the building. Is the building purpose-built or is it a building that has been converted from another building?

All the information can then be written up and presented to the rest of the school in an assembly, making use of short descriptions, paintings and drawings.

Prayer

Father God we have seen the importance of sharing a meal in the Gurdwara. Make us ready to share with those who do not have enough to eat. Amen.

Hymn

No. 74 'Sad, puzzled eyes of small hungry children' in *Come and Praise 2*, published by BBC, London, 1988.

3   Friends

Jonathan and David

The teacher should encourage the children to discuss:

(a)   What they would like to give their best friend as a symbol of their friendship.
(b)   What they have actually given to their best friend.

The answers could be shared in front of the whole school. If a dozen children work in pairs, one child could tell his best friend what he would like to give his friend, money no object; and the other child could say what he has actually been given. This needs very careful handling and preparation. If the whole class is involved in the exercise, the teacher should carefully select those children who have given precious gifts, rather than those who have been given merely expensive gifts i.e. a conker on a piece of string, or a football card, or a beautiful marble, in order to explain that expensive gifts are not necessarily the most precious.

Then a group of children could act the story of Jonathan's and David's friendship.

You will need the following characters and props:

Characters	*Props*
King Saul	Cloak
David	Armour
Jonathan	Sword
Boy Servant	Belt
Chorus	Spear
Narrator	Pile of stones
	(made out of cardboard)
	Harp

Narrator: Do you remember the courageous story of how David killed the giant Goliath? Well, King Saul wanted to know who the young boy was and employ him in his service.

King Saul: Who are you young man?

David: I am David, the son of Jesse, Sir.

King Saul: I want you to work for me, you have proved to be very brave and courageous. I want you to meet my son Jonathan, he is about your age.

Jonathan: I am Jonathan. David, you have shown such courage and bravery, that I want to be your friend forever. As a sign of my friendship, I will give you my cloak, armour, sword and belt.

[He puts each item on David.]

David: Thank you Jonathan. I, too, will be your friend forever. Nothing will ever spoil our friendship.

Narrator: David became so successful on all the King's expeditions, that the King made David an officer in his army.

Chorus: Saul has killed thousands, but David has killed tens of thousands.

Narrator: Then a very sad thing happened. The King became so jealous of David that he wanted to kill him. You see, the people were singing and praising David for his successes in battle, and King Saul was very afraid that the people would make David King, instead of himself.

Chorus: Saul has killed thousands, but David has killed tens of thousands.

Narrator: One day when David was playing his harp, the King threw his spear at David and tried to kill him, but the spear missed David by inches. King Saul told his son Jonathan, that he was going to kill David, but, because Jonathan loved David, he told his friend to hide, until he could make his father see sense.

[The actions are mimed in the background]

Jonathan: David, my friend, you must go away and hide, until I can stop my father from trying to kill you.

David: I do not know why your father wants to kill me, but I will do as you say.

[David goes off-stage]

Jonathan: Father, why are you trying to kill David, he has never done you any wrong. On the contrary, he has done nothing but good. Look how he saved us all from the Philistines by killing the giant Goliath.

45

King Saul: Yes, I suppose you are right, but I am afraid David will take the throne away from you, my son. But because of you, I will not kill him.

Chorus: Saul has killed thousands, but David has killed tens of thousands.

Narrator: But King Saul did not keep his promise. He sent his men to kill David in his bed. David's wife overhead the plot to kill David, and helped David to escape. She put a bundle of material in the bed, so that the men would think it was David. When the King found out, he was furious. David went to find his friend Jonathan.

David: What have I done to your father? Why does he want to kill me?

Jonathan: I'm sure he doesn't want to kill you, really. Look, I'll tell you what we'll do. We will make a plan. You go and hide in that large field behind that pile of stones. I will bring my servant into the field to collect the arrows that I shoot. If I shout out that the arrows have fallen *in front* of the stones, you know that you are quite safe and that my father does not want to kill you. But if I shout out that the arrows have gone *beyond* the stones, you will know that my father *does* want to kill you and so you must run away and escape. It is the New Moon festival tomorrow, and if you are not at our dinner table, my father will notice. I will say that you have had to return to Bethlehem. Now look, hurry and do what I say, go and hide.

Narrator: So David went and hid in the field and Jonathan went off to his father's house for the feast. King Saul asked where David was and Jonathan said that David had returned to his home town of Bethlehem. The King was furious and said that as long as David lived, Jonathan would not be king. So King Saul said that he would kill David. Just as Jonathan had promised, he took his servant with him to the fields to shoot arrows. He called out in a loud voice.

[The action is mimed]

Jonathan: Boy, run and fetch my arrows, look they have gone *beyond* those stones.

Narrator: The boy fetched the arrows but could not understand why Jonathan had said that the arrows had gone beyond the stones, because they were in front of the stones. However, he did as he was told and picked up the arrows. Then Jonathan sent the boy back to the city. When he was safely out of the way, he called to David to come out of hiding.

[The action is mimed]

Jonathan: You can come out now, my friend, it is quite safe. But you must get away from this place, you were right, my father does intend to kill you.

Narrator: So Jonathan kept his promise and protected David. They hugged each other and said good-bye. They promised that inspite of their difficulties, they would always remain friends.

[The action is mimed]

King Saul pursued David and tried to kill him many more times, but David always managed to escape. Until one day, when David crept up on King Saul, as he was resting in a cave, and he cut off a piece of the King's cloak, to show the King, that he could have killed him, but that he had spared the King's life. When King Saul heard this from David, he broke down and cried, and he said:
    'You are more worthy to be King than me'. So eventually David was crowned King.

[The action is mimed in the background]

The teacher needs to draw the threads together by emphasising the fact that Jonathan's love for his friend, David, saved David's life. Could we be such a true friend in the face of parental opposition?

Prayer

Father god, we thank you for the gift of friendship. Help us not to quarrel or break friends. Help us to be quick to make friends again after an argument. Amen.

Hymn

No. 35 'Take care of a friend', *in Every Colour Under the Sun*, published by Ward Lock Educational.

5–11
Assembly
Islam

Muhammad Shows a Way to Remain Friends

(It should be noted that when speaking Muhammad's name, Muslims pay respect to him, by saying the words 'Peace be upon him.')

The Ka'aba in Makkah is the most sacred shrine of Islam. It is a cube-shaped building which has stood in the centre of the great mosque's courtyard in that city for many centuries. It is believed to date back to the time of Ibrahim. Muslims, during Hajj or pilgrimage, always walk around the Ka'aba seven times and touch or kiss the Black Stone which is set into one corner.

Traditionally, it is believed that the stone, then white, was given to Ibrahim by the Angel Jibra'il. It turned black with all the sins of the world. It is very sacred to all Muslims.

There is a story told about Muhammad and the Black Stone, which showed his wisdom in dealing with people and helping them to avoid strife.

In the Sixth Century, the Ka'aba was flooded and had to be rebuilt. The rebuilding work began, and when it was nearly finished, the moment came when the black stone had to be re-set into the wall of the Ka'aba.

There were many eminent Arabian chiefs helping with the work and they each felt that they should have the honour to replace the stone. They argued and grumbled about who was the most important amongst themselves and therefore, who should have this honour.

Tempers flew, nerves became tattered and everyone shouted and argued at once. First one chief pushed forward and then another, and another and another and so on, all claiming to have the right to do the honours. Eventually, one chief said, 'Since we can not decide who should have this honour, let us wait and ask the first person who comes to the Ka'aba so settle our dispute'. The first person to walk through the courtyard that very moment was Muhammad.

Once again voices rose in anger as various chiefs tried to explain the problem to Muhammad, and each laid claim to the honour of replacing the stone.

Muhammad was absolutely silent for a moment and the noise died down, as everyone waited expectantly for Muhammad to choose the most favoured person. In a strong voice Muhammad asked for a sheet to be brought to him. 'A sheet, a sheet', the word whistled around the perplexed onlookers. Eventually, a sheet was found and brought to Muhammad. He told all the chiefs to take hold of the sheet and carefully edge the stone into the middle of it, without touching the stone. The chiefs did as they were told and soon the stone was safely in the middle of the sheet. Then Muhammad told the chiefs to raise the sheet to the level of the wall where the stone was to be replaced and to gently ease it into position. This they did with great care and the stone fell into place in exactly the right spot. As the chiefs lowered the sheet they were all beaming and smiling and shaking hands. Muhammad had turned a ferocious argument into a moment of friendship. How wise he was. Could we turn a problem like that into a solution?

Prayer

Almighty God, help us to turn difficult situations into pleasant ones, arguments into friendships. Amen.

5–7
Assembly
All

Making-Up
(Indian Folk Story)

(Adapted from *The Oldest and The Wisest* by T.C. Collocott in New Radiant Readers 5, published by Allied Publishers Limited)

One of the most difficult dilemmas for young children is the problem of making friends again after a quarrel. A quarrel seems devasting and irrevocable to a young child, and he/she needs to learn that making friends again is one of the basic rules for living. This story demonstrates the point.
    You will need the following:

Characters
        An Elephant
        A Monkey
        A Pheasant
        Narrator

Props
        Elephant Mask and Long Trunk
        Monkey Mask and Long Tail
        Pheasant Mask and Wings

Narrator: Once upon a time there were three friends; [Enter friends] an elephant, a monkey and a pheasant. Now these three friends, had been friends for a very long time. They lived and played happily together. The elephant used to give the monkey rides on his back; [Mime the action] and gently spray the pheasant with water, so that she could clean her feathers. [Mime the action] The monkey would find luscious fruit and share it with his friends [Mime the action] and the pheasant would make sure that the flies did not bother her two friends, by flapping her wings to keep them away. [She mimes the actions]
    They all lived together in peace and contentment for many years, helping each other and chattering happily. But one fine day, as they lay under the shade of a large banyan tree, they started bickering and quarrelling.

Elephant: Oh do stop, chattering monkey, there is a time for talking and a time for resting and you never stop talking, and I want to rest.

Monkey: Oh shut up elephant, you are always complaining. I shall chatter if I want to. Who is going to stop me?

Pheasant: Stop arguing both of you, I'm trying to have a pleasant dust-bath and all I can hear is your incessant quarrelling.

Elephant: Well, that's another thing, you are spraying dust into my eyes pheasant, so why don't you go somewhere else and have your bath?

Narrator: The three friends went on arguing and arguing until it nearly ended in fisticuffs. Then nobody spoke to each other, they moved away from each other and sulked. Thankfully, it was elephant who saw some sense and told his friends to come back together again, as he had a plan for making up. Reluctantly, with long faces and dragging their feet, monkey and pheasant came back to elephant and asked him about his idea.

Elephant: Well, it's like this. If we can decide who is the oldest of us all, that person shall rule over the other two, and we shall all do as he says.

Monkey: Alright, but how do we know who is the oldest?

Pheasant: Well, we have lived under this banyan tree, all of our lives. Whoever can remember the tree at its smallest, must be the oldest.

Elephant: Well, I can remember when it was about this high, because I can remember stepping over it.

[Shows height with his foot]

Monkey: Well, I can remember when it was *this* high, because I can remember nibbling the top of it.

[Puts his hand down lower than elephant's foot]

Pheasant: Well, I can remember when it was only a seed, because you see, I planted it.

Elephant: Well then, you must be the oldest, so we will all do whatever you say.

Monkey: Yes, we will.

Narrator: But pheasant was not only the oldest, she was also the wisest, because she had a plan of her own.

Pheasant: Well, I may be the oldest, but I think it would be wise if we all try to live peacefully together. Let us speak honestly with each other and agree that if something annoys one of us, we must try to stop doing it. Let us always say we are sorry if we upset one another. But the other person must be ready to forgive and forget and make friends again quickly, should we happen to quarrel. We could try putting an arm around each other or rather a wing and say sorry, let's forget it.

Elephant: Yes, I will try, I could put my trunk around you two.

Monkey: And I could curl my tail around you two.

Narrator: So, once again the friends lived in peace and contentment. Occasionally, they quarrelled as friends often do, but they remembered the wise advice of the pheasant, and quickly forgave each other and forgot about the past by putting a comforting trunk, or wing or tail around each other.

Prayer

Father God, forgive us when we quarrel with our friends and help us to make friends again quickly, by forgiving and forgetting. Amen.

Hymn

No. 31 'Thank you for my Friends,' in *Tinder-Box: 66 Songs for Children*, published by A. & C. Black.

The First Brotherhood

This is the story of five courageous men, who, when it came to the crunch, were willing to die for their Guru. It was Guru Gobind Singh, the tenth Guru, who put his followers to the test, in the month of Baisakhi. The date in 1699, was 30th March, but this story is now celebrated everywhere by Sikhs on 13th or 14th April, (due to calendar changes over the years).

In 1699, Guru Gobind Rai (as he was then known) was at Anandpur in Northern India. There was great danger of war breaking out between the Sikhs and the Mogul rulers, who were trying to convert the people to Islam.

The Sikhs were not ready for battle and Guru Gobind Rai was afraid that many would lose their lives unless they were organised into a disciplined, respected band of people, a force with which to be reckoned.

Some Sikhs, object to their Guru being portrayed in drama and so it is wise to check with the local Sikh community before enacting the following play. (Piara Singh Sambhi suggests that the Guru's part could be spoken from inside the tent or by the narrator.) Assuming that there are no objections, *you will need the following*:

Characters
> Guru Gobind Rai
> Daya Ram (a warrior)
> Dharam Das (a farmer)
> Mukham Chand (a washerman)
> Sahib Chand (a barber)
> Himmat Rai (a potter)
> Group of sikh followers
> Narrator

You will needs the following props:
> A tent
> A sword (with red paint on it to signify blood)
> 6 saffron robes with blue sashes
> 6 turbans

Narrator: (The Narrator sets the scene) Many Sikhs had gathered together at Anandpur and were worried and afraid that there would be a war.

Sikh Group: (All talking at once) What shall we do? Who shall lead us in battle? How shall we maintain our faith?

Guru Gobind Rai: [Emerges from his tent wearing a saffron robe with a blue sash and a turban, the crowd quietens down expactantly.] Is any one here willing to die for me to show his allegiance to me? [Silence] Who will give me his head as a sign of obedience to my leadership? [Silence] Is no-one willing to die for me, to prove he is a true Sikh?

Daya Ram: Leader, I am willing to lose my head for you.

Guru Gobind Rai: Come with me then.

Narrator: The two men entered the tent and everyone heard a cry, a thud and then the Guru returned alone with his sword blood-stained. Everyone was frightened and quiet.

Guru Gobind Rai: Now, is anyone else willing to die for me?

[He asks the question three times.]

Dharam Das: Take me, Teacher, I am willing to die for our cause.

Narrator: Once again the two men entered the tent, and once again, the people heard a cry, a thud and the Guru returned alone with his sword covered in blood.

Guru Gobind Rai: I need a third person to die for me. Who is willing [The crowd cowers] come along, someone must be willing to lose his life, if I ask it. Who will step forward?

Mukham Chand: I am willing to lose my life, Sir.

Narrator: Once again the Guru took the man into his tent and the same sounds were heard and the Guru emerged alone.

Guru Gobind Rai: I can see by your faces that you are all afraid, but three men have been brave enough to die for me, and now I want a fourth man to show courage. Is anyone else brave enough to die for me? Surely someone is? Who will step forward?

Sahib Chand: Take me, Teacher, I will do whatever you ask.

Narrator: For a fourth time, the two men disappeared inside the tent, and the same sounds were heard and the Guru stepped out alone.

Guru Gobind Rai: Now I want one more man to die for me. Is there anybody else?

Sikh Group: No, no, [gasps, muttering] No, no. Enough, enough.

[Some of the crowd run away.]

Himmat Rai: I am willing to die. Take me.

Narrator: Once again the two men went into the tent and the same sounds were heard. Then all of a sudden, the tent doors were thrown wide open and the five men emerged wearing new saffron uniforms, sashes and turbans.

Guru Gobind Rai: These men were willing to die for me. They had more courage than all of you. They are, indeed, very brave men. I shall call them my 'Beloved Five'. They are my true friends. If anyone else wants to show their bravery and courage and loyalty to me, they must drink this amrit (a mixture of sugar and water). All men who drink this amrit must change their names to Singh (which means lion) and all women must change their names to Kaur (which means princess). This is to show that we are united and courageous and that we will be respected. I, too, will take the name Singh. Henceforth, I shall be known as Guru Gobind Singh and we will be a force with which to be reckoned.

Prayer

Almighty God, make each one of us brave and courageous, so that when things are difficult, we can face up to them with new boldness. Amen.

Hymn

No. 50 'When a knight won his spurs in the stories of old', in *Come and Praise*, published by the BBC, London, 1988.

4   Clothes and Artefacts

**5–11
Assembly
Sikhism**

Clothes We Wear

Sikh men are proud to wear their turbans, as it clearly identifies their religion, as followers of Guru Gobind Singh, the last human Guru. It is important to emphasize to children that wearing a turban is a sign of strength, living like their Guru, and that Sikhs all over the world have campaigned to be allowed to wear their turbans in all sorts of occupations, where traditionally helmets or other head gear would have been worn i.e. the Police Force.

The turban covers the Sikh's uncut hair, and can be cloth of different colours.

It was Guru Gobind Singh who formed the Khalsa or brotherhood of Sikhs (see pages 53–55). Each Sikh who wishes to become a member of the brotherhood must possess the five special symbols known as the five Ks. They are known as such, because each item begins with the letter K in Punjabi.

The first, as we have already seen, is the Kesh or uncut hair. This means uncut facial and body hair too. Beards are folded up in a special way, so that they look neat and tidy. Hair on the head is kept in place by the second K, the Kanga or comb, that is worn beneath the turban.

A bracelet is worn on the wrist. This is called the Kara. A small sword is worn over the shoulder, and this is called the Kirpan. Where jobs or work places prohibit the wearing of the sword, Sikhs have worn a small replica of a sword set into the kanga or comb.

Finally, men wear the kaccha or shorts underneath their trousers.

Sikh women also wear kaccha, and they must always dress modestly. To this end, many women and girls wear trousers or shalwar, and a tunic called a kameez. Some women wear saris, but all women cover their heads with a beautiful piece of material like a long, flowing headscarf called a chunni.

For this assembly, it would be helpful if one of the dads could demonstrate how a turban is tied or, if there are no Sikh families available to help, teachers could write to The Sikh Missionary Society (UK), 10 Featherstone Road, Southall, Middlesex UB2 5AA.

This society will send teachers the names and addresses of their nearest Gurdwara or meeting place and perhaps the name of one of the members, who would be willing to come into school to demonstrate the wearing of the turban. (see picture on page 214).

Perhaps the visitor could also show the children the five special Ks and tell them why they wear each one. Each has a special significance. Briefly, it is this. Holy men in India did not cut their hair, so the uncut hair reminds Sikhs to keep their lives holy. The comb reminds the wearer to keep his hair clean and tidy and this must be reflected in orderly living. 'The kara or bracelet is made to protect the sword arm '(*Sikhism*, Piara Singh Sambhi, published by Stanley Thomas, 1989.) and 'reminds Sikhs that God is one, without a beginning or an end' (*The Sikh World*, D. Singh and A Smith, published by Macdonald, London 1985, page 20). The kirpan or sword reminds Sikhs to defend their beliefs and to protect the weak; and the kaccha or shorts were suggested by Guru Gobind Singh, for ease in battle. Sikhs wear them today, as a reminder that they are still warriors.

If a visitor cannot come to the school, allow a group of children to dress up in their own five Ks, but remember that members of the real Khalsa have to make solemn promises before they are allowed to wear these symbols of their faith, and the items should be treated with dignity and respect (see part 10).

Prayer

Holy God, who has no beginning and no end, teach us to respect the beliefs of one another. Amen.

Hymn

No. 146 'We ask that we live and labour in peace' in *Come and Praise 2*, published by the BBC, London, 1988.

5–11
Activity/Assembly
Hinduism

Jewellery for a Hindu Bride

The greatest treat for all the children in a school assembly, would be to see and touch, the beautiful jewellery worn by a Hindu bride on her wedding day. This is often spectacular, and many children would never have seen such precious ornaments. Much discussion, art and craft work could be stimulated by inviting a Hindu bride into school to show the children her wedding outfit and jewellery.

Jewellery is worn on the head, in the nose and ears, around the neck, wrists and ankles and on the arms, hands and toes. 'The very prestigious piece of jewellery called "Vaijayanti", a special decoration worn by some Hindu brides today, is named after the necklace of Lord Vishnu'. (*A Hindu Family in Britain* by Saurest Ray, published by Religious and Moral Education Press, Exeter, 1986, page 71).

Apart from the sheer beauty of the gold and silver jewellery the patterns on the jewellery itself, would provide another area for study. Animals, birds, flowers and many Holy symbols may be represented on the jewellery.

After the assembly, let the children draw, paint and make jewellery of their own. The older children may like to research the designs, and record their findings, whilst younger children could describe what they have actually seen.

Prayer

Father God, thank you for beautiful things, shiny things and jewellery made out of precious metals. How lovely it is to admire the skill of the craftsman and the ability of the designer. We acknowledge you to be the perfect designer of all things. Thank you for these lovely patterns. Amen.

Hymn

No. 109 'Thank you for the summer morning', *in Come and Praise 2*, published by the BBC, London, 1988.

Clothes

It is important to discuss dress worn by a particular faith community, in order that others may understand and show respect for different forms of dress. It is particularly important for Muslims to dress modestly and to cover their whole bodies. This has implications for teachers in schools, who should not, for instance, ask girls to change for PE.

In discussing Islamic dress, it should be remembered that there are certain strict rules that Muslims follow. For instance, men may not wear silk or jewellery made of gold. Colours should be sober, as bright colours are seen as a distraction when praying or visiting a mosque. Women in Pakistan cover their whole faces, whilst most women in Britain cover their heads, and some still partially cover their lower face.

Women and girls from the subcontinent of India generally wear shalwar, a type of baggy trousers, which are tight around the ankle, and a kameez, which is a kind of long tunic.

Men in Pakistan, India and Bangladesh wear a similar outfit to the women, but usually, it is white in colour i.e. white trousers, white tunic and a white cap. In Britain today, whilst some men still wear their traditional costume, many men wear dark suits.

It should be noted that as Muslims come from many different countries, they have different customs and clothes; the above information applys mainly to the subcontinent of India. The Arabs, Kurds, Africans etc. have different styles of dress. Find a world map, and let the children make a class book about the traditional dress of each country where there are Muslims. Travel brochures may help.

Prayer

Almighty God, we have learnt this morning about the importance of dressing modestly. May this virtue always be reflected in our lives and in our relationship with others. Amen.

Hymn

No. 61 'All over the world', in *Come and Praise* published by the BBC, London, 1988.

7–11
Assembly
Buddhism

A Robe for a Theravāda Buddhist Monk

Children may have seen Theravāda Buddhist monks and nuns wearing their bright orange robes, and Tibetan monks wearing maroon, and Zen monks wearing black robes, so it is important that some explanation is given as to why traditional dress has been abandoned for a simple robe.

A simple robe is the practical, outward expression of the Buddha's teaching. 'The Buddha taught in the Four Noble Truths that being selfish and wanting things for yourself is a cause of suffering. Monks learn to want nothing for themselves. They live with only what they need, not what they want. Their needs are simple: food, clothing, medicine and shelter'. (M. Patrick, *Buddhists and Buddhism*, published by Wayland, East Sussex, 1982 page 30).

Traditionally, the colour was orange or saffron, because the saffron dye was readily available. Monks today, however, will wear black or yellow or maroon robes depending on their particular tradition.

The monk wears his robe as a sign that he has renounced material possessions and intends to live simply by what he is given. Monks also shave their heads and go about barefoot.

It is important to note that the Theravāda monk folds his robes in a specific way. The four main folds in the front represent the Four Noble Truths:

1 Suffering is a part of life.
2 Suffering is due to selfishness
3 Suffering will stop if selfishness is overcome
4 The way to bring suffering to an end is to follow the Eightfold Path.

(M. Patrick, *Buddhists and Buddhism*, page 10).

The Eightfold Path is as follows:

1 Accept the Four Noble Truths
2 Think in the right way which leads you to help others
3 Be kind in speech, avoid boasting, gossip and lies
4 Do what is right

5 Earn your living in a way which is good
6 Avoid evil thoughts and actions and work hard
7 Learn to meditate
8 Be at peace in your mind.

(M. Patrick, in *Buddhists and Buddhism* page 11). See also pages 183–186, section 10.

So it can be seen that by wearing the robe, the followers of the Buddha are portraying his precepts. Ideally, for this assembly, a Theravāda Buddhist monk or nun should be invited into school to show how the robe is worn, and how the four folds are positioned to represent the Four Noble Truths. (If a non-Theravāda monk is invited, the details will be different). The teacher can write to the Buddhist Society, who will supply the names and addresses of the nearest Buddhist Monastery or Speaker. (see address below).

Prayer

Father God, help each one of us to be selfless rather than selfish. Help us not to be greedy, but give to others. Help us never to gossip or tell lies. Teach us always to do the right thing. Help us to work hard and live peacefully. Amen.

Hymn

No. 143 'I've got peace like a river', *in Come and Praise 2*, published by BBC, London, 1988.

Address:
The Buddhist Society,
58, Eccleston Square,
London SW1V 1PH

5   Festivals

7–11
Assembly
Judaism

Sukkot

Build a sukkah (a small hut) for the Jewish Harvest Festival of Sukkot.

The school indoor or outdoor climbing frame would be ideal for building a sukkah. Sukkot (plural of sukkah) takes place in the Jewish month of Tishri, about the same time as Christians celebrate Harvest Festival.

Jews often build their sukkah (or tabernacle) in their gardens, or decorate a special garden shed with all sorts of harvest gifts like oranges, and apples, and grapes. The roof, although covered with branches, should be open to the sky as a reminder to the Jewish people of the tents in which their ancestors camped, during the forty years they spent wandering in the wilderness, over 3000 years ago.

Many families today build their sukkah not only to thank God for His goodness in providing the food we eat, but also as a reminder that God has taken care of His people throughout history. The festival lasts for eight days and Jewish families try to eat many of their meals outside in their tabernacle.

There are four important symbols related to Sukkot. The first is the etrog or lemon. The second is the lulav or branches from a palm tree. The third is a branch of myrtle and the fourth, a willow branch. There are many interpretations of these symbols, one might be to represent the four elements, fire, air, earth and water, respectively. These symbols are then tied together and carried by the worshippers as a reminder of the good things that God has provided. The worshippers then point the branches in every direction showing God's goodness is all around us.

Perhaps four children could hold up the symbols and say in turn what they represent. Then the whole school could learn Psalm 117 and say it together:

Psalm 117
Praise the Lord, all nations!
Praise him, all peoples!
His love for us is strong
and his faithfulness is eternal.
Praise the Lord!
(From the Good News Bible)

Activity

Divide the class into four groups representing earth, wind, fire and water. Simple costumes could be made to indicate each element, i.e. Flaming headdresses for fire; strips of blue/green crêpe paper hanging from shoulders to hands for water; green leaf-shaped hats for earth; and filmy sheets of chiffon for wind.

Let each group say who they are and how they help people and then dance or move to their piece of music. (Suitable pieces of music can be found on 'Classics 100' by K-Tel). End with a simple prayer.

Prayer

Thank you God for all your precious gifts to us. Especially for the good earth, the wind, fire and water. Amen.

Hymn

Sing the song 'Hoshana' *in Shalom: Songs for Children from the Jewish Tradition*, translated and explained by Andrea Baron, or sing 'Hodu L'Adonai Ki Tov' in *Sephardic Songs of Praise*, by Abraham Lopes Cardozo published by Tara Publications.

Hodu L'Adonai Ki Tov

This is from the Hallel (Praise), Psalms 113–118 which are sung, among other times, on Sukkot, Pesah and Shavuot. (See pronunciation guide in part 10.) This is part of Psalm 118.

> *Hodu l'Adonai ki tov, ki l'olam hasdo.*
> *Yomar na Yisrael, ki l'olam hasdo.*
> *Yomru na weyt aharon, ki l'olam hasdo.*
> *Yomru na yirei Adonai, ki l'olam hasdo*

> Thank the Lord, for He is good,
>   for His love is everlasting.
> Let Israel now say:
>   'For His love is everlasting.'

Let the house of Aaron now say:
'For His love is everlasting.'
Let all who fear the Lord now say:
'For His love is everlasting.'

Hannukah or the Festival of Lights

You will need the following:
Judah Maccabee
Jewish Army
Syrian Army
Temple Dancers

Props:
Swords
Hannukah menorah or eight-branched candle, plus one for lighting, making 9 altogether (a home-made one would do. This could be done by placing 9 candles in pots or jars).

Explain to the children that over two thousand years ago, Judah Maccabee led a small band of Jewish people into battle against the Syrians, who had spoilt their Temple and had tried to stop the Jews from worshipping God.

The drama can commence with a battle between two groups of children portraying the Jews and the Syrians, fighting each other with swords. The Temple dancers, representing the pagan worshippers, dance in and out of the Temple in the background. Judah Maccabee is pronounced the victor. The small Jewish army take back their Temple, banishing the dancers [who go and sit down] and then worship God.

[The Jewish army kneels in prayer]

Judah lights the first Temple lamp (the menorah) as a symbol of God's presence, and then discovers that there is only enough of the precious oil to last for one day. He dispatches a group of people to get more oil, but whilst they are gone, by some miracle, the oil lasts for eight days.

Judah now lights the other seven candles in turn.

Explain that Jews today light the special Hannukah menorah in remembrance of the eight days that the oil lasted. The Festival takes places in December. Presents are given on the first day and special food, that has been cooked in oil (like doughnuts) and latkes (potato cakes) are eaten. Try to obtain an eight-branched candle to show the children. The Temple menorah has seven branches, it has become a symbol for the Jewish people everywhere.

End the assembly with a simple prayer.

Prayer

Heavenly Father, thank you, that we can still worship you today, freely. Help us to keep your commandments of old. Amen.

Hymn

'Love one Another', (Leviticus 19: Verse 18) in *Songs and Hymns of Fellowship*, published by Kingsway Publications or 'How Many Candles?' (origin unknown).

How Many Candles

A counting song for Hannukah: sing up to 'one' on the first night, up to 'two' on the second night and so on up to eight. It can be very meaningful to sing *while* lighting a Hannukiyah (with a shamash or 'helper' candle). (A.W.)

> *How many candles, how many candles,*
> *How many candles do we light?*
> *On our hannukiyah, on our hannukiyah*
> *On this Hannukah night?*
>
> *(Chanting) one, one, one, one, one, one*
>
> *One candle burning, one candle burning,*
> *One candle burning bright*
> *On our hannukiyah, on our hannukiyah*
> *On this Hannukah night.*

Chorus: How ma - ny can - dles, how ma - ny can - dles,
Verse: One can - dle burn - ing, one can - dle burn - ing,
Two
Three,etc.

How ma - ny can - dles do we light?
One can - dle burn - ing ___ bright.

On our ha - nu - ki - yah, on our ha - nu - ki - yah,
On our ha - nu - ki - yah, on our ha - nu - ki - yah,

On this Ha - nu - kah ___ night.
On this Ha - nu - kah ___ night.

One, one, one, one, one, one.
Two, two, two, two, two, two.
Three,etc.

**5–11
Assembly
Judaism**

The Festival of Purim

The Festival of Purim or the Feast of Lots is celebrated in the Jewish month of Adar around February/March time. The teacher will find the account in the Bible. But it is best read from a children's bible or an abridged version. It is called the Feast of Lots, because Haman cast lots to 'choose the best day on which to kill all the Jews' (Esther chapter 4, Verse 7, *Good News Bible*).

You will need the following:
> King Ahasuerus of Persia
> Three Advisers to the King
> Queen Vashti and hand-maidens
> Esther and servant girls
> Hathach (Esther's man-servant)
> Haman (The King's Prime Minister)
> Mordecai (Esther's Uncle)

Props: Two crowns
> Gold sceptre (which the King lifts as a sign to enter his presence)
> Greggers or rattles (made from plastic bottles filled with rice to be used as shakers)
> Labels (to be hung round the neck of each character and briefly introduced before the play begins).
> Beautiful cloak
> Ring

As the story is read aloud by the Narrator, the children mime or act their parts. The rest of the school can shake their rattles or hiss every time Haman's name is mentioned and cheer at the end for Queen Esther. Each class may like to wear fancy dress to school for the performance.

The story goes like this:

Narrator: King Ahasueras summons Queen Vashti to his banquet, but she refuses to obey.

King: Come to my feast

Queen Vashti: No!

King: Call my Advisers. [Advisers enter] The Queen has insulted me, what shall I do with her?

Advisers: You must banish her, and make another girl Queen.

Narrator: So the advisers find a young Jewish girl called Esther. They bring Esther to meet the King. She kneels before him.

King: Esther, you shall be my Queen. I will give you this crown to wear.

Narrator: Haman enters. The audience can hiss and shake rattles.

Haman: I am Haman, the King's Prime Minister. I'm so important that everyone must bow down to me.

Narrator: The servants and advisers bow down. But Mordecai, Esther's uncle remains standing.

Haman: But who is this, who refuses to bow down to me?

Mordecai: My name is Mordecai. I am a Jew. I only bow down before God.

Narrator: Haman was so angry that he went to the King and this is what he said:

Haman: O King dear [hiss] there are some very wicked people in your kingdom, who do not obey your laws. You must sign this proclamation to put them all to death. Yes, men, women and children. Kill them all. And not only will you rid yourself of these wicked people, but also you will become very rich because you can take all their gold and silver as well. So do sign here [Hiss] King dear.

Narrator: So the King agreed and signed the proclamation. When Mordecai, Esther's uncle, heard the news, he was so upset and cried out loudly. [Mordecai wails loudly] The Queen's servant girls heard Mordecai crying and told Esther, so she sent her trusted servant Hathach to Mordecai. Mordecai told Hathach about Haman's wicked plot and begged Esther to go to the King, but Esther said that if anyone went to the King without being invited, they were instantly put to death. However, she sadly agreed.

Esther: I will go to the King, and if I am put to death, so be it. But you and all our fellow Jews must pray for me and eat nothing for three days. My servant girls and I will do the same. Then I will go to the King.

Narrator: On the third day, Esther put on her best clothes and went to see the King. He raised his golden sceptre, which meant that she could enter his throne room.

King: Why dearest Esther, what do you want? You can have anything you want, you know, even half my kingdom.

Esther: Your Majesty, will you and your Prime Minister Haman come to a special banquet tonight?

[Hiss]

King: Of course, we will come.

Narrator: A wonderful feast was prepared and the King and Haman arrived.

[Hiss]

King: Now my Queen, you can have anything you ask for. What do you want?

Esther: Will you and Haman come to dinner again tomorrow night?

[Hiss]

King: Of course, we will come.

Narrator: Haman's friends advised Haman to build a special platform on which to kill Mordecai. But that same night, unknown to Haman, the King remembered that Mordecai had saved his life, and so he ordered Haman to give Mordecai a beautiful cloak to wear. Haman was furious. [Hiss. He puts the cloak on Mordecai] The next night, the King and Haman went to Esther's banquet.

King: Now my dearest Queen, what do you want from me?

Esther: My Lord, I ask you to spare my life and the lives of all my people.

King: What on earth do your mean? Who says you must be killed? Show me the man who says such a thing.

Esther: This evil man, Haman says so.

[Hiss, boo, shake rattles etc.]

King: Take him away at once and hang him. And bring Mordecai to me, he shall be my Prime Minister.

[Mordecai enters and kneels before the King. The King gives him his ring]

Esther: Please stop your proclamation to kill all my people.

King: I'm afraid the order has already been sent out, but Mordecai can write to all the Jews in all the provinces and warn them to defend themselves.

Narrator: So there was much joy and happiness because the Jewish people were saved. Mordecai and Queen Esther said that the people must remember this day forever and have a festival on the same day every year. Lets give Queen Esther a cheer.

End by singing the Purim songs below, and let each class, in turn, parade round the hall to show off their Festival Fancy Dress.

Prayer

Thank you Lord for the bravery of Queen Esther and for showing that you are against tyrants. Amen.

Songs

'Purim' in *Shalom, Songs for Children from the Jewish Tradition*, translated and explained by A. Baron; or 'Ani Purim' in *Sefer Hamoadim Vol. 6*, Ed. Yom-Tov Levinski published by Tel-Aviv, Agudat Oneg Shabbat, 1955; or 'Der Rebbe', a traditional Yiddish East European Folk Song.

Ani Purim

Purim is a time for silliness and this is a silly song! Masks, fancy dress, street parades, clowning and all-round humour are an effective response to antisemitism: laughing prejudice in the face. (A.W.)

> *Ani Purim, Ani Purim sameah um'vadeah.*
> *Halo rak paam bashanah avo l'hitareah.*

> *My name is Purim, Purim, Purim, festival of gladdness.*
> *I only visit once a year (Ha, ha, ha) so throw away your sadness.*

* Here there can be a short break in the song for a burst of laughter.

Der Rebbe

It is a custom for anyone who is so moved to act as Purim Rabbi for the day. This light-hearted Yiddish song about 'The Rabbi' is Purim-ish in spirit. Whatever the Rabbi does, it says, his Hasidim also do. (A.W.)

En az der rebbe   *zingt (La, la, la) zingen alle die Hasidim. (La, la, la)*
                    shluft (snore) shlufen (snore)
                    veynt (oi, oi, oi) veynen (oi, oi, oi)
                    shveygt (silence) shveygen (silence)
                    dovt (ruh, ruh, ruh) doven (ruh, ruh, ruh)
                    klept (clap) kleppen (clap, clap, clap)

When the Rabbi   sings (La, la, la) all the Hasidim sing (La, la, la)
                 sleeps (snore) sleep (snore)
                 weeps (oi, oi, oi) weep (oi, oi, oi)
                 is silent (silence) are silent (silence)
                 prays (ruh, ruh, ruh) pray (ruh, ruh, ruh)
                 claps (clap, clap, clap) clap (clap, clap, clap)

5–11
Assembly
Judaism

Pesah or Passover

This exciting story can be found in the Bible, in Exodus chapters 5–12. However, the teacher needs to summarize the main events and retell the story in her own words.

The story provides a marvellous opportunity for dramatic movement, accompanied by music from home-made instruments.

Opportunities for children to wear frog, locust, gnats and fly masks, are afforded, as children act out the plagues sent by God in order to persuade the King of Egypt to let the Israelites go free.

The beat of hailstones, the whisper of death, the eery sounds of darkness covering the land, the rushing water of the red sea, can all be musically interwoven into the story.

Then the Passover meal itself. The Jews of old were told by Moses to mark their door-posts with lamb's blood, so that the Angel of Death would pass over their homes, thus sparing them the death that was intended for the Egyptians.

Every year since then, the Passover meal or Seder is commemorated by Jewish families, the world over. The meal takes place on the first evening of this seven day Festival in the Spring. (See picture on page 175).

The table is set with various special items as a reminder of what Passover means. For instance, Matzot or Unleavened bread is eaten as God commanded. Lamb is roasted and eaten with bitter herbs (Horseradish) (see Exodus, chapter 12, verse 8).

For the assembly, choose a Narrator to tell the story, and divide the children into groups representing the different plagues, the Jewish people, the Egyptians, animals and dancers, and then let the children mime their parts as the story is retold.

The Passover Play

You will need the following characters:
    Moses
    Aaron
    King of Egypt
    King's Advisers
    Frogs
    Gnats

Flies

Locusts

Various animals (cattle, sheep, horses, camels etc).

Hailstones (children dressed in white shifts with paper balls to throw)

Darkness Dancers (children dressed in black tights and leotards)

Narrator: Moses goes to the King of Egypt and asks him to free the Jewish people from slavery.

Moses: The Lord God of Israel, says, 'Let my people go'. (Good News Bible)

King: No. I will not let your people go. They must work for me, making bricks. I will beat them and make them work harder.

Narrator: Moses spoke to God and told him that the Jewish people were even worse off than before. God promised to set His people free and told Moses to go back to the King.

Moses: You *must* let my people go, or God will turn this River Nile into a river of blood.

Narrator: The King refused, so Aaron (Moses' brother) held out his stick over the Nile and the river turned to blood. But still the King refused to let the people go.

[Two children waft a long piece of red material into the air to represent the river of blood see suggestions for dance music on page 82]

Moses: Let my people go, or the Lord God will send a plague of frogs to cover your land.

Narrator: But still the King refused to let the people go.

[Frogs leap and jump all round the hall]

Moses: Let my people go or the Lord God will send a plague of gnats all over your land.

Narrator: But still the King refused to let the people go.

[Gnats dance round the hall making snapping movements with their mouths]

Moses: Let my people go or the Lord God will send a swarm of flies over your kingdom.

[Flies buzz round the hall.]

Narrator: But once the flies had gone, the King refused to free the people again.

Moses: Let my people go, or the Lord God will send a dreadful disease that will kill all your sheep, cattle, donkeys and camels.

[Sheep, cattle, donkeys and camels stand up and walk round and then gradually fall to the ground, dead]

Narrator: But still the King refused to let the people go.

Moses: Let my people go or the Lord God will send a plague of boils on all your people.

[Boils are quickly painted or stuck on the King's face and the faces of his advisers]

Narrator: But still the King refused to let the people go.

Moses: Let my people go or the Lord God will cause a heavy hailstorm to fall on the country, such as you have never seen before.

Narrator: Thunder, lightning and hailstones struck the ground.

[The children can make a cacophany of sound with their instruments at this point]

King: Alright Moses, this time I have had enough, I will let your people go.

Narrator But once the hailstorm stopped, the King changed his mind.

Moses: Let my people go, or the Lord God will send as swarm of locusts to eat up all your crops and destroy all your trees and fill all your homes.

[Locusts swarm round the hall pretending to eat everything]

Narrator: But once the locusts went away, the King still refused to let the people go. So God sent a terrible darkness over all the land which lasted for three whole days and nights.

[Eerie music may be played by the children. Other children wearing black tights and leotards do a darkness dance]

King: Alright, you may go this time.

Narrator: But the King went back on his word once more and refused to let the people go.

Moses: Let my people go, or the Lord God will send *one final* punishment on you and all your people. He will kill all your first born children, including your *very own* son.

Narrator: God told Moses to mark the door post of the homes of all the Jewish people, so that when the Angel of Death passed through Egypt, He would not harm the Jews. This was done, but the Angel of Death killed all the first born sons of the Egyptians including the King's *very own* son. Then the king sent for Moses once more.

King: Get out of my country, you and all your people. Leave at once, go and worship your God, and leave me alone in peace. I have had enough. I can't bear any more.

Narrator: So the Jewish people left quickly, taking with them unleavened bread to eat (i.e. dough that has not had time to rise, because of the need for speed) bundles of clothes and the gold and silver given to them by the Egyptians. And God told Moses that the Jewish people must hold a Passover Festival every year in remembrance that God had set them free.

The assembly could end quite simply at this point with the hymn and prayer below, or the next episode, crossing the Red Sea could be retold and re-enacted.

Prayer

Father, we pray for all people everywhere who are bullied or teased by others. Help us, in our own small way, to right any wrongs that we see. Amen.

Hymn

Sing the Passover Hymn 'He is Lord of All' in *Shalom: Songs for Children from the Jewish Tradition*, translated and explained by Andrea Baron, Address on page 177.

Some Suggestions for Dance Music for the Pesah Story

(Taken from the double cassette tape entitled *Essential Classics*; *33 of the Greatest Classics* by Polygram Record Operations Ltd.)

River of blood Orff 'Carmina Burana' — O Fortuna (Side 3 no. 1)

Frogs Johann Strauss 11 'Emperor Waltz' Extract (Side 2 no. 5)

Gnats Vivaldi 'The Four Seasons' — Spring — First Movement (Side 1 no. 4)

Flies Wagner 'The Ride of the Valkyries' (Side 3 no. 3)

Sheep die Massenet 'Thais' — Meditation Extract (Side 3 no. 2)

Thunder and Lightening Sibelius 'Karelia Suite' — Intermezzo (Side 4 no. 3)

Locusts Bizet 'Carmen' — Prelude (Side 3 no. 5)

Death Mahler Symphony no. 5 — Adagietto (Side 4 no. 6)

(Modern, popular music can be used just as effectively)

Kathina

This Theravāda Buddhist festival takes place in October and November. It is a time when gifts are given to Buddhist monks before the onset of winter.

The tradition started during the Buddha's life-time. A group of monks were making their way, in July, to spend their annual retreat season with the Buddha. They did not arrive in time and so were obliged to spend the three-month retreat apart from him. When the retreat was over, the Buddha suggested that they make a new robe together, as a unifying, compensatory activity. People round about willingly gave cloth and dye and a frame called a Kathina, on which to stretch the cloth to make the new robe.

Since that time, it has become the custom to give cloth for new robes to the monks in Buddhist Monasteries. Many other basic necessities are also given to the monks and nuns during this festival.

The day begins early, with people arriving at the monastery. The Three Refuges and the Five Precepts are chanted:

I go to the Buddha for Refuge
I go to the Dharma for Refuge (Teaching)
I go to the Sangha for Refuge (Order of Monks)

(M. Patrick, *Buddhists and Buddhism*, published by Wayland, East Sussex, 1982, page 25).

The Five Precepts are the rules by which Buddhists promise to live:

1   Not to destroy or harm life
2   Not to steal
3   Not to commit adultery or have irresponsible sexual relations
4   Not to tell lies
5   Not to take intoxicating drinks or to take drugs

On this festival day, there follows a communal meal and the offering of gifts takes place. The cloth is then made into a robe and the festival ends when the finished article is presented to the chosen monk.

For this assembly, all this historical information can be given to the children, followed by an activity in empathy with the tradition of making and giving.

With so many natural disasters throughout the world, it would be a worthwhile activity to make a blanket or bedcover to be sent to one of the disaster areas perhaps bearing the name of the school. A quick and easy activity is for everyone to knit a square of wool that can be joined together to make a colourful blanket. The teacher could ask everyone at the assembly to contribute.

Prayer

Father God, help us to give joyfully to others in need. Amen.

Hymn

No. 31 'Because you care', in *'Every Colour Under the sun'*, published by Ward Lock Educational.

Diwali

(See part 10 for a guide to pronunciations)

This important Festival of Light, reminds Hindus of the triumph of good over evil; light over darkness. It can be seen in the story of Ram and Sita triumphing over the evil demon king.

The festival takes place around October/November time. For many Hindus, this festival marks the Hindu New Year, although there are other New Year festivals in different regions of India. Greeting cards are sent to family and friends; visits are made to relations, gifts and sweets are exchanged. Diva or small lights are lit and placed in all the windows of the houses as a reminder of the triumph of light over darkness.

The story of Ram and Sita can be retold or presented as a drama or puppet play. It can be retold in the following way:

You will need the following characters:
Narrator
Ram — Handsome Prince
Sita — Beautiful Princess
Ram's Father — The old King
Ram's Step-Mother — The old Queen
Bharat — Ram's half-brother
Lakshman — Ram's other half-brother
Vulture — The King of the Vultures
Ravan — The Demon King with ten heads
Old Beggar — The Demon King in disguise
Monkeys — Who help Ram and Sita
Hanuman — The leader of the monkeys

The Narrator introduces each of the characters in turn.

Narrator: This is Ram, the handsome Prince

[Ram puppet takes a bow]

This is Sita, his beautiful Princess wife

[Sita takes a bow]

This is Ram's father, the old King.

[King bows]

This is Ram's step-mother, the old Queen.

[Queen bows]

This is Lakshman, Ram's half-brother.

[Lakshman bows]

This is Bharat, Ram's other half-brother.

[Bharat bows]

This is the Vulture King. [Vulture king bows]
This is Ravan, the Demon King. You can hiss when he comes on to the stage.

[Ravan bows. Children hiss]

Finally, this is Hanuman and the monkey army. You can cheer.
Now we are going to tell you a story about all these characters.

[Enter the old King and Queen]

Queen: Listen my dear King, I think my son Bharat should be the next King, and not your son Ram. I think you should send Ram away for a while.

King: I don't want to send Ram away, but I will send him out into the forest to fight many battles and prove that he is worthy of being the next King.

[King and Queen exit. Enter Sita, Ram and Lakshman]

Sita: If you are going away from the Palace Ram, I am coming too.

Ram: No you can't come with me — it will be too dangerous.

Lakshman: Well, I am coming with you. I can help you fight your battles and I will look after you and Sita if you let her come.

Ram: Well, all right, you can both come, but I warn you, we have a very difficult journey ahead of us and I don't know what danger will befall us.

Narrator: Ram, Sita and Lakshman set off. Suddenly, Sita sees a beautiful deer and and begs Ram to capture it for her. Ram sets off to catch it, and tells Lakshman to remain behind and look after Sita. But Lakshman thinks he hears Ram cry out for help, so he says to Sita:

Lakshman: Wait here. I will draw a circle in the dust around you to protect you — on no account must you speak to anyone or step outside this circle. I must go and help Ram.

Narrator: Sita agreed, but suddenly, whilst the two men were gone, an old beggar came up to Sita and begged her for some food. He was really the Demon King in disguise.

Beggar: Please give me some food.

Sita: No I can't, I promised not to step outside this circle.

Beggar: But if you don't give me some food, I shall surely die.

Sita: Oh all right then, just for a moment, here is the food.

Narrator: In an instant, the Demon King changed back into King Ravan with ten heads and captured Sita. The King of the Vultures heard Sita's cries and tried to help, but Ravan was too strong for him, and struck him to the ground with his sword. Ram and Lakshman returned, and saw that Sita had gone and the Vulture King lay wounded on the ground.

[The action is mimed]

Vulture: Oh Ram, the Demon King Ravan, has taken away your beautiful wife, I tried to stop him, but he struck me with his sword.

[Enter Hanuman and monkey army]

Narrator: Just then Hanuman, the Monkey King, and his army of monkeys came by, and Hanuman promised Ram that he would help him find Sita. Everyone searched and searched, calling out her name. At last Hanuman discovered where she was being held prisoner. She was on the island of Lanka. Hanuman went to find King Ravan.

[The action is mimed]

Hanuman: You must let Sita go, or else there will be a fierce battle and you will surely die.

Ravan: Ha, ha, no-one is strong enough to kill me. To teach you a lesson I am going to set fire to your tail.

[Children hiss]

Narrator: Poor Hanuman's tail was set alight, but he lept from building to building, burning the houses with his tail as he went. In the meantime, the monkey army, who had built a bridge across the sea from India to Lanka, arrived and came to help their King fight Ravan. After a fierce battle, it was Ram who killed Ravan with his spear. Ram, Sita and Lakshman returned home, where Ram was crowned King and Sita was crowned Queen by Bharat, Ram's other half-brother.

[The action is mimed. Children can cheer]

Hymn

No. 62 'Diwali', *in Tinder-box*; *66 Songs for Children*, published by A. & C. Black.

Ravan, the Demon King

Source: Ann and Bury Peerless – Slide Resources and Picture Library

Diwali

Sikhs as well as Hindus, celebrate Diwali, or the Festival of Light, but for different reasons. As we have seen on pages 85–88 Hindus remember the story of Ram and Sita, and good triumphing over evil. Sikhs remember a very important event in their own history, the release of the sixth Guru, Guru Hargobind from prison. However, both festivals are celebrated at approximately the same time of year in October/November. As Sikhism developed out of Hinduism, it is natural that Sikhs have retained some of the Hindu festivals, and the release of Guru Hargobind, actually occurred at the time when the Hindus were celebrating Diwali, in the year 1620.

This lovely story of the Guru's ingenuity, could be re-enacted by the children. However, it is important to remember that some Sikhs do not like to see their Gurus portrayed in drama, and so it is as well to seek approval from the local Sikh community before performing the following play. If there are objections, Piara Singh Sambhi suggests that the part of Guru Hargobind could be spoken by the narrator or from behind a curtain. The reason for this, should be explained to the children.

You will need the following:

Characters
> Guru Hargobind
> Muslim Emperor, Jehangir
> 52 Hindu Princes (10 could be a representative number)
> First Prince
> Second Prince
> Third Prince
> Sikh followers (10 or more)
> 2 Prison Officers
> 2 children to make an archway
> Narrator

Props
> Hargobind's cloak (with tassels)
> Bundle of Food

Narrator: (The Narrator sets the scene) This is a story that happened a long time ago. The Muslim Emperor Jehangir, had been told that the Sikh Guru, Guru Hargobind, had attracted many followers and that the Guru had built a fort in the city of Amritsar. He was afraid that the Guru might plot against him and try to kill him, so he decided to have Guru Hargobind thrown into prison at a place called Gwalior.

Emperor Jehangir: What is all this I hear about you building a fortress at Amritsar, is it true?

Hargobind: Yes Sir.

Emperor: So you are plotting to kill me, are you, and to take my place as Emperor?

Hargobind: No Sir, of course not.

Emperor: I don't believe you, throw him into jail.

Narrator: Poor Hargobind was taken by two armed prison officers and thrown into jail.

[Prison Officers come forward and push Hargobind into jail]

Narrator: Once inside the jail, Hargobind looked around him and found that there were many others there, accused of the same crime. In fact there were fifty-two Hindu Princes all wanting to talk at once.

Princes: [All talking at once]
Look here,
Let me tell you,
Did you know,
We are so badly treated etc. etc.

Hargobind: Stop, stop, I can't hear you, if you all talk at once. Will somebody tell me why you are here, and why you are so angry?

First Prince: We are so badly treated. We are not even given enough food to eat.

Hargobind: Well then, you must have some of mine. Some of my friends gave me this bundle of food, please take some and share it, all of you.

Narrator: So the princes sat down and shared the food between them.

[Group sit in a circle and the bundle is passed around]

Hargobind: Now, will someone tell me why you are here?

Second Prince: We are all accused of plotting to kill the Emperor.

Third Prince: And it is all untrue.

Narrator: Hargobind listened to their grievances and day by day, he continued to share his food with them. Many days went by, and Hargobind was still kept a prisoner, even though he was innocent. Each day, more and more of his Sikh followers came and stood outside the jail in a silent protest about his imprisonment.

[Sikh followers get up, one by one, and form a semi-circle around the group sitting in the jail]

Narrator: The prison officers began to get worried about this and decided to go and see the emperor.

Officers: Your Highness, we do not know what to do, we fear that there will be a riot, unless you free this man Hargobind. Every day, more and more of his followers are standing outside the jail.

Emperor: Let me look into his case, and see if I can release him. It may be better for all concerned, if I set him free.

[He shuffles through some papers]

Well, looking at these papers, the case against him seems a bit thin. Perhaps we had better let him go.

Officers: Yes Sir, thank you Sir, we will go and tell him at once.

Narrator: So the officers left the emperor and hurried to tell Hargobind that he was free.

Officers: Hargobind, we are here to tell you that the Emperor has set you free. You can leave right now.

Princes: [Together] What about us? What about us? Set us free too. Why can't we leave? This is unfair. It's unjust. It's criminal.

Hargobind: Thank you for your message from the Emperor. But please, will you tell his Highness, that I cannot possibly leave prison, without my fifty-two friends here.

Officers: He won't like it, he won't like it, you know. He will be very angry and may not release *any* of you.

Narrator: However, the officers went back to tell the Emperor. [The officers and Emperor put their heads together and mutter.] Then the officers return to the jail.

First Officer: Hargobind, the Emperor has said you may go, and as for these princes here, the Emperor will only free those princes, who can pass through this narrow doorway with you, at the same time as you leave. Only those princes who can actually touch your clothes, will be released with you. Ha, ha, ha, they will have to be jolly thin to pass through this doorway with you. Ha, ha, ha.

Narrator: The Guru, bowed with thanks and called all the princes together. Then he spoke again.

[The action is mimed]

Hargobind: I am now ready to leave, officer, and so are the princes who are coming with me.

[Hargobind stands up and passes through the archway made by the two children holding their hands together. As he does so, he un- does his cloak and each of the princes grasp hold of a tassle and so passes through the archway]

Officers: [Scratching their heads] Well I'm blowed. Well, we can't stop them, they *are* touching the Guru's clothing, but who would have thought that this could happen?

Narrator: So the Guru and the princes all passed through the archway to freedom. The Guru went back to Amritsar and saw many little lights or divas lighting up the fortress. Today, Sikhs everywhere light divas as they remember this lovely story about their Guru.

Prayer

Holy God, help us to see the needs of others as well as our own, and to always be ready to help others in distress. Amen.

Hymn

No. 127 'Diwali time is here', *in Come and Praise 2*, published by the BBC, London, 1988.

5–11
Activity
Hinduism

Navratri (or Nine Nights) and Dussehra

(Pronounced Nav/ra/tri; first 'a' is short; the second 'a' is long as in far'; 'tri' rhymes with 'see'. Duss/eh/ra, 'Duss' rhymes with 'thus', 'e' as in let, 'ra' rhymes with 'far'. See Part 10 for further guide to pronunciations.)

The festival of Navratri and Dussehra is celebrated by Hindus all over the world, during late September or early October. The mother goddess or devi is worshipped, and the triumph of good over evil is celebrated. The festival takes different forms in different parts of India.

In one of her many forms, the mother goddess is called Durga, and she is depicted defeating the demon king. During each of the nine nights of the festival, Durga's different powers are remembered, culminating on the tenth night or Dussehra, with a terrific bonfire, on which the huge effigy of Ravan, the Demon King, is burnt. (See pages 85–88 for the story about Ram and the Demon King).

Indeed, in some parts of northern India, the emphasis is not so much on the goddess Durga, as on the victory of Ram (the incarnation of Lord Vishnu) over the Demon King Ravan. The story is retold and re-enacted, culminating with Ram defeating Ravan. There are great bonfires and firework displays.

But the message is much the same, goodness triumphs over evil, and many Hindus use the festival time, as a time of rejoicing and goodwill.

The festival provides a wonderful opportunity for art and craft work in school. The children could either make a huge effigy of the demon king for a bonfire of their own, or make the mother goddess Durga, with her ten arms. (It should be noted that it takes years to train a proper sculptor to make the mother goddess, as skills are handed down from generation to generation. Sculptors adhere strictly to the guidelines in the Hindu Scriptures).

Prayer

Almighty God, we remember that this festival commemorates goodness triumphing over evil, may this be true, both in our own lives and in our schools. Amen.

Hymn

No. 134, 'I planted a seed', in *Come and Praise 2*, published by the BBC, London 1988.

The goddess Durga

Source: Ann and Bury Peerless – Slide Resources and Picture Library

7–11
Assembly
Islam

Ramadan and The Festival of Eid-ul-Fitr

Ramadan or the month of fasting, is a very important month in the Islamic calendar. It is the ninth Islamic month and Muslims believe that it was during this period, that the Angel Jibra'il spoke the sacred words to Muhammad, who ordered them to be written down and later collected as their Holy Book, the Qur'an. (See Part 10, for a note regarding the date of the festival.)

During the hours of daylight, Muslims must not eat or drink anything. The fast begins when the new moon is seen at the beginning of the month and ends when the new moon is seen at the end of the month. Muslims can have a drink and a meal from sunset to dawn but not during daylight. Very young children and old or sick people are excused the fast. Muslims keep this time as a reminder of what it is like to be poor and hungry and because God commands it in the Qur'an.

At the end of the period, the Eid-ul-Fitr Festival is held. It is a time of great joy and feasting. New clothes are bought, cards and presents are sent to friends and relations, and money is given to the poor. But the day always begins with prayers at the Mosque.

Prayers are always preceded by the usual pattern of washing. Hands, mouth, nose, face, arms, head, ears, neck and feet must all be washed before the prayers can begin. Every Muslim has to learn the set pattern of prayers and prayer positions and must face towards Makkah (Mecca). (See pictures on pages 122–126) Shoes must be removed as a mark of respect for God. Women pray in a special part of the Mosque, away from the men.

There are three aids to prayer that are used; a prayer mat, (obligatory) prayer beads to remind Muslims of the 99 names for God in the Qur'an, and a compass to show the direction of Makkah.

Prayer

There is a video cassette about prayer available from the Islamic Cultural Centre and Central Mosque
146, Park Road,
London
NW8 7RG
Tel: 071–724–3363–7

Eid-ul-Adha

(See Part 10, for a note regarding the date of the festival)

This is the festival that takes place at the end of Hajj or pilgrimage in the twelfth month of the Muslim calendar. If they can, each family, will sacrifice a sheep or cow, giving part of it to families who cannot afford to make the sacrifice. This is done, in remembrance of Prophet Ibrahim's willingness to sacrifice his son, Isma'ail. Isma'ail was the son born to Ibrahim and Hagar. Muslims believe that Ibrahim was a great Prophet who was asked by Allah (God) to sacrifice his son as a test, to demonstrate his willingness to obey Allah in everything. (The story can be read in the Qur'an or in the Bible. If the story is read in the Bible, it is Isaac who is sacrificed and not Isma'ail. See Genesis chapter 22, verses 1–19. In the Qur'an it is chapter 2 verses 126–128 and 37 verse 102).

There is a problem over presenting this exciting story in dramatic form, as Muslims are not allowed to present God or his Prophets as persons. Therefore, out of respect for the Muslim people, the story should be simply retold by a story-teller.

One day, when Ibrahim was alone, he heard Allah speaking to him in a dream. Allah asked Ibrahim, if he was willing to be completely obedient to Him, in every detail of his life. Of course, being a righteous man, Ibrahim told Allah that he would do anything that Allah asked him to do. So Allah put Ibrahim to the test. He told Ibrahim to take his son to the land of Moriah, where Allah would show him the place where Ibrahim must sacrifice his son.

Poor Ibrahim was devastated, but he knew he must obey Allah. The next morning, he cut up some firewood and took his son to the place that Allah had told him about. Ibrahim told Isma'ail what Allah had asked him to do, and Isma'ail said, 'O my Father, I do that which thou art commanded (Qur'an, 37:102). Sadly, Ibrahim looked at his beloved son, and he ordered him to lie down on the wood, ready to be sacrificed. He was just about to kill Isma'ail, when suddenly Ibrahim heard the Angel Jibra'il's voice, telling him not to touch or harm the boy. The Angel Jibra'il told Ibrahim, that God knew now, that Ibrahim, was completely obedient to Him in all things, and as a reward, Allah would richly bless Ibrahim. God provided a sheep for the sacrifice. Ibrahim quickly untied his son, and sacrificed the sheep instead. Ibrahim invited everyone to share in the festivity.

That is why, at the festival of Eid-ul-Adha, families sacrifice a sheep or cow in memory of this event, and they give part of the sheep away to the poorer families, who cannot afford to make their own sacrifice. This shows God's provision for them too.

Prayer

Almighty God, help us to be obedient to you, in all our doings. Thank you for providing for all our needs. Amen.

Holi — The Hindu Festival of Colour

(See part 10 for guide to pronunciation)

This is a riotous festival that marks the beginning of Spring. People/revellers squirt coloured water or paint at each other. The festival takes place during March.

One way of expressing this riotous celebration of colour in class is to squirt paint onto a huge sheet of paper and then allow the children to make a massive, collective finger painting.

This then, can be pinned up and shown to the rest of the school. The class can show the children how they can dance to the movement of the paint; pretending to be the squiggles and swirls and explosions of colour. (This is far 'safer' than squirting paint at one another in school!)

The story of Holika and Prahlad can be retold (see part 10 for further information).

Prayer

Thank you God for the return of Spring and for all that this means to us. Thank you too, for the joys of festival and the promise of new life. Amen.

Hymn

No. 98 'You shall go out with joy', in '*Come and Praise 2*', published by the BBC, London, 1988.

7–11
Activity/Assembly
Sikhism

Hola Mohalla

As we have already seen on page 99, this was a Hindu festival. But the tenth Guru, Guru Gobind Singh, wanted Sikhs to have their own celebration. So in 1700 C.E. he introduced the festival of Hola Mohalla in Anandpur, in the foothills of the Himalayas.

The festival was to be a time when all Sikhs gathered together to celebrate all kinds of sports and gamesmanship; Guru Gobind Singh wanted a time to display the strength and ability of his army. So with this in mind, he arranged displays of 'swordsmanship, horsemanship, archery and wrestling competitions'. (J.G. Walshe, *Celebrations across the Cultures*).

Today, too, Sikhs continue to celebrate Hola Mohalla by having athletic tournaments and other sporting events such as horse riding. The festival is still celebrated in Anandpur, in rememberance of Guru Gobind Singh's command to meet together for this Spring festival. Today, in the West, after the sporting events, Sikhs usually go to their Gurdwaras and pray for health and strength and the ability to keep their bodies fit.

For this assembly, groups of children could display their prowess in mock sword fights, wrestling, gymnastics etc. Perhaps the importance of keeping one's body healthy, could be stressed. It might also be a good opportunity, to warn the children against smoking, drinking and drug abuse. Perhaps a small group of children could research these topics and present some statistics in graph form, written work and art work. Close the assembly with a simple prayer.

Prayer

Father God, help each one of us to keep our bodies fit and healthy. May we never abuse our bodies by drug abuse. Amen.

Hymn

No. 16 'For all the strength we have', in *Someone's Singing Lord*, published by A. & C. Black.

6   Rites of Passage

5–9
Assembly
Hinduism

A Hindu Naming Ceremony

In Hindu culture there are lots of different ceremonies for naming a baby. Ceremonies may differ for a variety of reasons. For instance, variations occur according to the caste into which the baby is born, or the region in which the family resides.

However, most Hindu babies' names are determined by their horoscopes. The Brahmin or family priest works out the child's horoscope from the exact moment that the baby was born. Then, based on this information, the priest will often choose the initial letter for the baby's name. Hindu names usually have a special meaning. For instance, if a boy's initial letter is 'R', he might be called Ram, after one of the gods. This naming ceremony usually takes place ten days after the baby is born, and it is a very special occasion when the baby is welcomed into the world.

For this assembly, having given the children the above information, hold a competition and write down as many names as possible beginning with a certain letter. Children from different cultures should be given the opportunity to explain the meaning of their names if they know it. Of course, many young children may not know the meaning of their name, and so this could become a project to be researched at home.

Once the children have understood the concept that calling people by their proper name is important, and that everyone is unique and valuable, perhaps the teacher could use the occasion to discuss the improper use of name-calling and so discourage prejudice of any kind.

Compare and contrast other name-giving ceremonies (see part 10.)

Prayer

Lord God, we thank you that each one of us is special and precious in your sight. Amen.

Song

'Today's a special day', in *Sing a Song of Celebration* by M. Martin and V. Stumbles, published by Holt, Rinehart and Winston.

Bar Mitzvah/Bat Mitzvah

Boys become Bar Mitzvah at around the age of twelve years. Girls become Bat Mitzvah at around the age of thirteen years. Bar Mitzvah means 'Son of the Commandments', Bat Mitzvah means 'Daughter of the Commandments'. Before boys and girls can take part in this joyful ceremony, they will have received special lessons from their Rabbi or teacher, and they will have had to learn how to read a special portion of the Scriptures. It is quite difficult.

Before the age of twelve or thirteen, the children's parents are responsible for their behaviour and actions; but at this special ceremony, the children, themselves, take on the responsibility for their own actions. That is, they promise to obey God's commandments and to keep the Jewish laws for themselves. They are considered to be old enough to judge right from wrong and to act accordingly. This is a turning point in the young people's lives; leaving childish behaviour behind and acting in a more grown up way.

For this assembly, it would be a good idea to invite a Bar Mitzvah boy or girl into school, to tell the children something about their studies, and perhaps read their special portion of scripture for the children, and discuss what it means to make their commitment in this ceremony.

The school children may not have seen a Tallit or prayer shawl; the Shel Rosh and the Shel Yad, the boxes that are worn on the head and arm, so these too, could be brought into school and shown to the children, together with the photographs of the Bar Mitzvah/Bat Mitzvah festive meal. (N.B. It should be noted that the prayer boxes or tefillin contain portions of scripture and therefore should only be shown to the children and not handled by them).

Prayer

Father, we pray that we too, may work towards being responsible for all that we say and do. Help us to have a real concern for others in our community, to support one another at home and at school. Thank you for our parents and teachers who have taught us right from wrong. In particular, we thank you for ... (name of Bar/Bat Mitzvah boy/girl) who has reached this important stage in his/her life. We ask your blessing upon him/her and his/her family. Amen.

Song

This is a joyous song which is often sung at weddings or Bar/Bat Mitzvah parties, from *Israel in Song*, compiled, edited and arranged by Velvel Pasternak, published by Tara Publications, Cedarhurst, N.Y.

> Hava nagilah, Hava nagilah, Hava nagilah, v'nis'm'cha!
> Hava n'ran'na, v'nis'm'cha!
> U'ru ... achim
> U'ru achim b'lev sameach!
>
> Come, let us have joy and happiness in it!
> Arise, my friends, with a joyful heart!

lyrics: M. Nathanson

Hassidic

A Sikh Wedding

Begin by comparing and contrasting a typical English wedding in a church with a traditional Sikh wedding in a Gurdwara.

Discuss the pros and cons of choosing a partner for oneself and of having a partner chosen by one's family. Ask the children if they have attended a wedding. Make a wedding scrapbook.

As a wedding is such a happy and colourful occasion, it would be more meaningful if a mother was invited into the school to describe her beautiful clothes and the important aspects of the wedding ceremony.

Deep red is the traditional colour of a bride's clothes in India, whether she is Hindu, Muslim or Sikh. Sikh women wear a tunic or frock called a kameeze which is a little longer than a mini skirt and shalwar, which are like trousers gathered in tightly at the ankles. She wears a dupatta or veil on her head which is made to match the kameeze.

The distinguishing feature of a Sikh man is his turban which may be of any colour; but orange or red is the preferred colour for weddings.

Perhaps it might be possible to re-enact a Sikh wedding using all the children in the hall as wedding guests.

The main elements of the wedding are as follows:

The young man and the male relatives of both couples meet at the Gurdwara.

The groom's father places a garland of flowers around his son's neck. The groom sits down.

Then the bride enters dressed in red, with her sister or friend or a female relative. She sits next to the groom.

The bride's father places a garland of flowers around the Guru Granth Sahib (or Holy book containing the Sikh scriptures) and one around the neck of both the bride and groom.

The most important part of the wedding is when the groom leads the bride four times around the sacred book.

A special hymn is sung which tells the couple that true happiness lies in devotion to God.

A prayer is said.

Other friends and relatives bring garlands of flowers to the happy couple.

The couple leave for a special wedding feast.

Perhaps every child could be given a small sweetmeat to taste.
End with a simple prayer of thanks for the joy of all weddings everywhere.

Hymn

No. 37 'If I had a hammer', from *Someone's Singing Lord*, published by A.
& C. Black.

The Buddha Teaches About Death

Death is a very difficult subject to deal with in an assembly, and yet some attempt must be made to cover this subject in order to reassure those children who are grieving over the loss of loved ones, and perhaps reassure others for the future. It could be argued that the subject is best left until the need for explanation arises, but equally it could be argued, that it is much better to have tackled the subject long before an actual death, which inevitably, will be charged with intense emotion.

This story at least, may open the doors for free discussion, and bring some understanding to a grieving child, at the necessary time.

The story is a dramatized version of how the Buddha dealt with a grieving mother.

You will need to prepare the children carefully beforehand, that they are going to see a play about a mother whose baby has died, and who goes to see the Buddha for an explanation.

You will need the following characters:

The Buddha
Mother (with dead baby doll in her arms)
First Villager
Second Villager
Third Villager
Narrator

Mother: [Weeping approaches the Buddha] Oh Buddha, Buddha, help me, help me, my baby has died. Why should this dreadful thing have happened to me?

The Buddha: My dear, all mankind, everywhere, must suffer at some time or other in their lives.

Mother: Oh, but I hurt so much inside, and I am so full of sadness that I know that I will never be happy again.

The Buddha: I can see you are suffering now. I too, feel your pain, as if it were my own, but one thing I know is true, everything passes in time, even your pain will pass in time.

Mother: I cannot believe you. You do not understand how I feel — nobody understands. [Weeps]

The Buddha: [Gently] My dear, will you do something for me?

Mother: [Between sobs] What do you want me to do?

The Buddha: Go back to your village and knock on every door that you come to. Ask each person firstly, if they have ever suffered and, secondly, whether as time passes, the suffering passes. When you have done this, bring me back a seed from every house, where there has *never* been any suffering of any kind.

Mother: I am sure no-one else will have suffered like me, no-one has spoken to me about suffering. I will bring you back many seeds, I know.

Narrator: So the weeping mother set off and did as the Buddha had asked her to do. She knocked on the door of the first house in her village.

Mother: I have lost my baby, I shall never get over her death, but the Buddha has asked me to collect a seed from each house where I find there has been no suffering. Will you give me such a seed? I am sure that you have never suffered.

First Villager: I'm afraid I cannot give you a seed. You see, my mother died when I was quite young and the pain was so awful. We all suffered. As children we helped each other in our grief, but we still suffered greatly. I cannot give you such a seed. However, one thing I can tell you, that as time passed, the pain has lessened and we are now able to talk about our mother without crying. We can even remember some of the lovely things that we did together and sometimes laugh. But we did suffer at the time.

Narrator: The mother hurried on to the next house in search of her seed.

Mother: My baby has died and I am suffering greatly. Have you ever suffered?

Second Villager: Oh we are suffering now, you see our pet dog died this morning and we cannot bear his loss. Perhaps one day, when we feel better we will have a new pet, but not now.

Narrator: The mother did not receive a seed from this family. She could see they were suffering too, in a different way, and so she hurried on to the next house to find her seed.

Mother: The Buddha has sent me to collect a seed from you, if you can tell me that you have never suffered any loss or pain of any kind.

Third Villager: Well, I am afraid you will have to try another house, because you see, I cannot give you such a seed. We have all suffered greatly. You see, we lost our grandad. Oh we loved him so much, he used to do so much about the house. The only thing I can tell you, is that the pain was terrible at the time, but it has passed a little now.

Narrator: The mother travelled on and on asking first at one house and then another. But everywhere she went, she learnt that what the Buddha had said, was true. Everyone had suffered in some way, but eventually all suffering passed away.

Prayer

Heavenly Father, we pray for all those who are suffering the loss of a loved one at the moment. Comfort them and heal their sadness. Amen.

Hymn

No. 140 'Lead me from death to life', in *Come and Praise 2*, published by BBC, London, 1988.

7   Water Themes

5–11
Assembly
Judaism

Jonah

An activity assembly to involve the whole class. Much topic work can be encouraged beforehand to do with the sea, ships, sailors, whales etc.

You will need the following characters:

	Props
God	Storm effects
Jonah	e.g. percussion instruments
Skipper	Cardboard ship
Sailors	Large fish
Large Fish	Crown
King of Nineveh	Dressing-up clothes
King's Courtiers	Swords
People of Nineveh	
Narrator	

Small groups of children can practise their parts beforehand i.e. the sailors could learn the sailor's hornpipe dance; the people of Nineveh could practise mock fights; the courtiers could do a courtier's dance.

Begin in the following way. The children mime their parts whilst the narrator reads the story.

Narrator: God spoke to Jonah.

God: I am very angry with the people in the city of Nineveh. They have turned away from my ways and they are very wicked. Go and tell them that they must say they are sorry and try to live better lives, or I shall destroy the whole city!

Jonah: I don't want to go to that evil place. I shall hide from God. I shall go a long, long way away from God. I know, I'll take a ship and go to Tarshish.

Narrator: So Jonah set off to find a group of sailors who would sail him to Tarshish. By some very good fortune, he came across a group of sailors practising their sailor's dance, in Joppa.

[Hornpipe music — sailors have a few minutes to show off their dance]

Jonah: Please take me to Tarshish. Here is my fare.

Skipper: All right, we are just about to set sail, come aboard.

Narrator: So the ship set sail with Jonah on board. But God caused a huge storm to arise, which tossed the ship high on the waves and threatened to sink the little boat. The sailors, terrified for their lives, began to throw their cargo overboard. Meanwhile, Jonah lay fast asleep below deck. But the skipper soon went and woke him up.

Skipper: What are you doing here fast asleep? Wake up and pray to your God to save us. Look it must be your fault that this great storm has come upon us. Who are you, where do you come from?

Jonah: 'I am a Hebrew, and I fear the Lord God of heaven who made the sea and the dry land.' (RSV)

Narrator: Then he told them about what God had asked him to do and how he had run away. The sailors became exceedingly afraid. The skipper spoke again.

Skipper: What must we do to save ourselves?

Jonah: You will have to throw me over-board.

Narrator: The sailors did not want to do this, but in order to save their ship and their own lives, they took hold of Jonah and tossed him into the raging sea. Immediately, the sea became calm and the storm died down and the sailors were very afraid. They knelt down and prayed to God. Meanwhile God sent a huge fish to save Jonah from drowning. The fish swallowed Jonah with one gulp.

[Fish swims across the stage and swallows Jonah]

Poor old Jonah had to stay inside the fish for three days and three nights, but then he prayed to God.

Jonah: Thank you God for saving my life. Now, whatever you ask me to do, I will do.

Narrator: So God caused the fish to carry Jonah to the safety of dry land and the fish spat him out onto the shore. Then God spoke to Jonah again.

God: This time Jonah, you must obey me, and go straight to the people of Nineveh, and tell them that unless they say they are sorry and stop doing all these wicked things, they will surely die.

Narrator: So Jonah set off for the city of Nineveh to warn the people that they must turn away from their wicked ways or they would be destroyed within forty days.

[People of Nineveh stand up and demonstrate mock fights]

Narrator: The King and his courtiers were having a party when they heard whispers of what Jonah had been saying.

[Coutiers dance, then the dance stops as each couple whispers in the ear of the next couple]

Narrator: So the King of Nineveh spoke.

King: Listen to me everyone, we must ask God's forgiveness for our sins and try to lead better lives. No more fighting, no more bad behaviour. I declare a day of fasting. We will go without food and drink and put on sackcloths, to show God that we are truly sorry, and we will beg God to forgive us. Perhaps then we will be saved.

Narrator: When God saw all this, he knew that they were indeed truly sorry, so he did not punish the people of Nineveh. But the story does not end quite there. Jonah felt very cross with God because God did not punish the people after all. But God explained to Jonah that he would always forgive people if they were truly sorry.

Prayer

Father God, forgive us when we do wrong things and help us to lead better lives. Amen.

Hymn

'Ose Shalom' in *Israel in Song*, compiled, edited and arranged by Velvel Pasternak, published by Tara Publications, Cedarhurst, N.Y.

Ose Shalom

A traditional refrain which rounds off many set liturgical passages, is a recurring motif in Jewish art and a popular chorus for youth groups' singalongs.

The alternative form — appearing below in brackets — is favoured by some progressive communities who wish to extend the prayer for peace beyond those present and beyond the Jewish community — to all people. (A.W.)

Ose shalom bimromav, hu ya'ase shalom, aleynu v'al kol Yisrael
(v'kol benei adam) v'imru Amen.

May he who makes peace in the highest bring this peace upon us and upon all Israel (and all the human race) and let us say Amen.

The music is arranged in two parts. The air could be taught to younger children. Older children might like the challenge of learning the second part.

The Money Tree
(A Chinese Traditional Tale Based on a Story by Ken Ma)

For this assembly you will need a deep tray of water, and two small tins of oil paint, (the type used for painting model aeroplanes) two straws, and two or three pieces of paper that have been cut to the size of the tray.

The aim of this assembly is to show the children that the oil paint will always float to the surface, and a print can be made by floating the paper on top of the water. This is called marbling, and each of the children can have a turn in their classrooms after the assembly.

To demonstrate the activity, take one of the straws, dip it into the paint, and swirl it around on top of the water in the tray. Do the same thing again, with the other coloured paint. Then simply float the paper on the top of the paint and water and show the beautiful pattern that the oil paint has made.

This exercise can be repeated several times, to show that the oil will always stay on the top of the water and make a pretty pattern.

Then tell the following Chinese traditional tale about how oil floating on water, saved a little chinese boy and his family from financial ruin. The story could be mimed as the teacher tells the tale.

A long time ago, in a far away country called China, a little boy called Chang, made his living for his family by selling oil, for people to use in their oil lamps.

Each week, when it was market day, Chang would carry his two cans of oil to market, carefully balanced on each end of a long pole that he carried on his shoulders. It was a very long walk to the market and the cans felt heavier with every step. But as soon as he got to the market he would set up his little stall and sell oil to everyone who came to him. It was quite a messy job, and the oil would often spill over his fingers as he poured it from his large cans into the little oil lamps that people would bring for him to fill up. People placed the money into his little oily hands and he put the money carefully into his pockets. When all the oil was sold, he would carry the empty tins back on his shoulders and start walking the long journey home.

On one particular market day, when he had been selling oil all day, he felt so tired that he decided to sit down and rest under an enormous shady tree, just outside the market. Before long, his eyelids began to feel very heavy and he fell fast asleep. He must have slept for some time, because when he awoke, most of the people had left the market place and they were going home. He picked up his empty cans, put his hands in his pockets to check that the money was still safe and made ready to set off for home. To his horror, he found that his pockets were quite empty, the money had all gone, it had been stolen.

Poor Chang burst into tears. He got down on his hands and knees and looked all round the base of the tree, just in case the money had fallen out of his pockets. But there was not a coin to be found. Chang put his head in his hands and cried loudly. What on earth would he tell his father? How could he tell him, that he had sold all the precious oil, and then lost all their money? He cried and cried.

Just then, an old wise man, with a very long beard, carrying a water jar and a walking stick, came along and asked Chang why he was crying. Through his sobs, Chang explained that someone had stolen all his money whilst he had been asleep.

'Oh' said the wise man, 'I know who has stolen all your money, it is this Money tree, under which you have been sleeping'. And taking his walking stick, he said, 'I will make the Money tree give it all back to you'. He set about hitting the Money tree to make it return Chang's money.

Very soon a huge crowd gathered around the old man and the young boy and when they asked what the old man was doing, they started to roar with laughter. 'There is no such thing as a money tree, you silly old thing. Why not beat the tree a bit harder, it might rain down jewels as well, or pearls, or gold. Ha, ha.'

When everyone had had a good laugh, the old man turned round and said 'You have been watching a show, and for making you laugh, you owe me two coins each'. Everyone stopped laughing, and tried to escape but the old man put up his stick and said, 'No-one leaves until you drop two coins into my water-jar'. One by one, the little crowd put two coins into the jar, when suddenly the old man shouted, 'Stop Thief'. A greedy, fat man looked at the old man, and said 'Who me?' 'Yes you,' said the old man, 'Come and look everybody, you can see for yourself that this man has stolen young Chang's money'. As the people crowded round the water jar, the coins had sunk to the bottom, but there was a strange oily film across the top of the water.

'Turn out your pockets at once', commanded the old man. Shaking with fear, the fat man put his hands into his pockets and produced all the missing coins, all covered in oil, by little Chang's oily fingers.

He had to give back all the money to little Chang and he was taken away quickly by a passing policeman. So you see, the oil floating on top of the water saved little Chang and his family from losing all their money.

Prayer

Father God, make each one of us completely honest. Help us never to steal anything that does not belong to us. Amen.

Hymn

No. 38 'Think, think on these things', in *Someone's Singing Lord*, published by A. & C. Black.

7–11
Assembly
Islam

The Importance of Washing before Prayers

For this assembly, encourage the children to think of all the ways that they can of keeping themselves clean, i.e. washing hands, feet, face, hair, bodies, teeth etc.

Talk about different methods of washing i.e. by having a bath, shower, a wash in a basin, under a garden tap, in the sink, or in a river, or in the sea etc.

Talk about the importance of washing in our daily lives i.e. washing dishes, cups, knives and forks, clothes, parts of the house like windows, floors, walls, all surfaces etc.

Think of washing outside i.e. cars, buses, streets, shop fronts etc. Encourage the children to think of nature and the importance of washing for birds, i.e. ducks, geese, and birds in bird-baths; and the different ways animals wash themselves, i.e. cats, rabbits, elephants, etc.

Try to emphasise the importance of keeping oneself fresh and clean in our daily lives, before telling the children about the purification washing ritual used by Muslims if they intend to pray. The Muslim washing ritual is called Wudhu, and in every Mosque there is a special ablutions area, in order to perform this duty. Explain too, that if a Muslim intends to pray at home, the same rules are applied. If a Muslim has had a bath or a shower, without the intention of washing for prayer, then the ritual washing of Wudhu must be done again even after a bath or shower. Muslims do this, because they were told to do so, by their Prophet Muhammad (Peace be upon him), and it is written in the Qur'an, the Muslim's Holy book.

Show the children the following series of pictures of ablutions and prayer positions and remind the children that a Muslim has to pray five times a day, so this ritual is repeated each time before prayers.

Adhan

The call to prayer.
Athan is uttered in a loud voice by the Muezzin (the caller) facing the direction of the Ka'aba in the following words, which are said in the order below.

1   Allahu Akbar
    i.e. 'Allah is Most Great' (four times).
2   Ash hadu an la illaha illallah
    i.e. 'I bear witness that there is no deity but God' (twice).
3   Ash hadu anna muhammadan rasullullah
    i.e. 'I bear witness that Muhammad is God's messenger' (twice).
4   Hayya 'alas–salah
    i.e. 'Come to prayer' (turning the face alone to the right and saying it twice).
5   Haya 'alal falah
    i.e. 'Come to success' (turning the face alone to the left and saying it twice).
6   Allahu Akbar
    i.e. 'Allah is Most Great' (twice).
7   La ilaha illallah
    i.e. 'There is no deity but God' (once).

N.B. The following phrase is added after item 5, in the Athan of the early morning prayer.; As-salatu khairun minan-naum i.e. 'Prayer is better than sleep' (twice).

Iqamat

Iqamat is the second call to prayer and is uttered immediately before the beginning of the Obligatory Prayer (fard). It is similar to Athan but with the addition of the sentence, Qad qamatis-salah
i.e. 'Prayer has indeed begun' (to be uttered twice after item 5, above).

Ablutions before Prayer and Prayer Positions
Copyright pictures and text are reproduced with the kind permission of Minaret House, 9 Leslie Park Road, Croydon, Surrey.

Ablutions before Prayer

1

Hands to be washed with water three times.

2

While washing the hands, water is to be applied between fingers.

3

The mouth is to be washed thoroughly with water three times.

4

While washing the mouth with water, the teeth are to be cleaned with the fingertip.

5

The nose is to be washed with water and blown three times.

6

The whole face is to be washed three times.

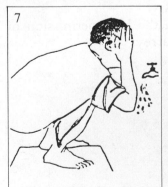

7

All parts of the face should be washed with water.

8

The right hand should be washed up to the elbow three times.

9

Then the left hand is to be washed up to the elbow three times.

10

To wash the arm thoroughly, this way should be followed.

11

The head is to be wiped with water.

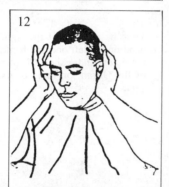

12

The ears are to be washed from the inside and the outside.

13

The right foot is to be washed up to the heel and ankle.

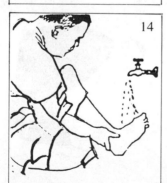

14

The left foot also to the heel and ankle.

Prayer Positions

15
The worshipper should face the
Qibla (Niche) with the inward
resolve to perform the prayers.
Then he has to raise his hands
on both sides of the face saying
"Allahu Akbar".

16
Then he should put the right
hand on the left one and recite
the Fatiha and a short Chapter
of the Qur'an, or some of its
verses.

17
The hands are again to be
raised on both sides of the face
and the words "Allahu Akbar"
should be uttered as the
worshipper prepares to bow.

18
The bow should be from the hips, so that the back
would be in straight horizontal posture. The hands
are placed, fingers spread on the knees and upper
parts of the legs. The worshipper silently repeats
three times "Glory be to my Lord, the Great".

19
When he straightens himself up after the bow, he should again raise his hands on both sides of the face and say"Allah listens to whoever thanks Him" followed by "Our Lord, thanks be to Thee."

20
Then the worshipper prostrates himself twice, with his nose and forehead placed on the ground between the palms of his hands.

21
While prostrating himself in prayer, the worshipper should straddle his hands and thighs, pointing the fingers and toes towards the Qibla. The worshipper repeats three times "Glory be to my Lord, the Highest."

22
Between the two prostrations, the worshipper should sit upright, saying "Allahu Akbar', putting his hands on his thighs near the knees.

23
When seated to recite Al-Tashahud (testimony), the worshipper, in the first sitting, should sit with the right foot upright and the left foot flat under him. In the second sitting of the final raka'a, he should put his left foot under his right leg, sitting on the latter and supporting himself on his bottom. This posture is known as 'Tawarrok'. During the recital of Al-Tashahud, when the worshipper says "I bear witness that there is no God except Allah," he should raise the forefinger of his right hand.

24
Then the worshipper should turn his head to the right, until his right cheek-bone may be seen, and say "assalamu alaikum wa rahmatullah."

25
He should then turn his head to the left, until his left cheek-bone may be seen, and say again "assalamu alaikum wa rahmatullah."

How the Kingfisher Got it's Name
(An Indian Folk Story)

(Adapted from 'How a Bird got its Lovely Colour' by S.G. Pottam in *Indian Folk Tales*, published by Sabbash Publishers).

You will need the following

Characters
> King
> Princess
> 4 Noblemen
> Brown Bird
> 4 Brown Babies
> Crow
> 4 black babies
> Narrator

Props
> Crown
> Ring
> Cloaks
> 5 Brown tunics of feathers and
> 5 Brown bird masks
> 1 Cloak of beautiful Kingfisher feathers
> 5 Black tunics of feathers
> 5 Black bird masks

Narrator: Once upon a time, two birds built their nests in the trees alongside the river Ganges. One was a little brown bird, and the other was a large black crow. [The brown bird and the black crow mime the building of nests and then sit down]. Very soon, both birds had laid four beautiful eggs each. They were both very proud of their eggs and showed them to each other.

> [The two birds mime twittering movements with their heads and beckon one another to come and look at each others eggs].

127

The black crow frowned and scratched her head. She thought that the brown bird's eggs looked distinctly nicer than her own. So one day when the little brown bird was diving in the river to catch fish to eat, the black crow did a most despicable thing. She very carefully swapped each of the brown bird's eggs with her own.

[The crow mimes the action whilst the brown bird pretends to dive for fish].

When the brown bird came back to her nest, she thought her eggs looked a little odd, but she settled down, and waited for her babies to hatch.

One fine morning, there was the sound of eggs cracking in the brown bird's nest, and out propped four large black birds.

[The action is mimed]

Brown Bird: Oh no, you cannot be my babies.

Narrator: Just at that moment, the eggs in the crow's nest began to hatch, and out popped four beautiful little brown birds.

[The eight children mime the action of breaking out of their eggs and make twittering movements around their 'wrong' mother]

Brown Bird: Crow, there must be some dreadful mistake, I have got your babies, and you have got mine. Please give me back my babies.

Crow: No, No, there is no mistake, these are my babies, I hatched them.

Narrator: Poor brown bird did not know what to do. Suddenly, she had a brilliant idea, she would go and see the King. Surely he could sort out her terrible problem. Brown bird flew off to the palace to seek justice, only to discover that the King had problems of his own. The Princess was in floods of tears, the King looked distraught, and the noblemen were going hither and thither searching for something.

[The birds leave the stage; the King, Princess and Noblemen enter]

Princess: Boo hoo, boo hoo, oh where, oh where can I have lost my ring? Are you sure that you have searched everywhere?

First Nobleman: I have looked all over the Palace.

Second Nobleman: I have looked everywhere in the gardens.

Third Nobleman: I have looked in all the fields.

Fourth Nobleman: The only place we haven't looked in, is the river. We need that little brown bird that dives into the river to catch fish. She could look and see if you dropped your ring in the river.

King: Bring the brown bird to me.

Brown Bird: I am here Sir, I heard everything, because I was coming to tell you, that crow has stolen my babies.

King: Well then, if you find my daughter's ring, I will give you a very great reward. But first, let us deal with your problem. Come on everyone let us go down to the river. I shall devise a test to sort out whose babies belong to whom.

Narrator: Everyone went down to the river, where crow was sitting with her brown babies.

King: Now, little black birds, I want you all to dive into the river to see if you can find my daughter's ring.

Narrator: The four black birds lined up and, one by one, jumped into the river. The first one, nearly drowned and came up coughing and spluttering; the second one put it's toe in the water and then ran away in fright. The third one dipped it's wing in the water, fell over, and came out shrieking and squawking; and the fourth one was so frightened at seeing all it's brothers' and sisters' mishaps that it held it's nose, closed it's eyes, flapped it's wings and took a running jump. It landed splat, on a stone and had to be helped up by everyone else.

[The four black birds mime these actions in turn]

King: Now come along, little brown birds, it's your turn. Line up, line up, see if you can find my daughter's ring.

Narrator: The little brown birds lined up beside the river and with one beautiful movement, they dived into the water and came up again.

[The baby brown birds mime the action and come up smiling]

Baby Brown Birds: We saw something beautiful and shining down there, but we haven't learnt to pick up things yet, we're so little.

Mother Brown Bird: But I can, your majesty, let me go and have a look.

Narrator: The brown bird dived into the water and sure enough, she came up holding the Princess's ring.

[The action is mimed]

King: Now it must seem clear to you crow, that these brown birds are not afraid of the water, and those black birds are afraid. You are a very silly mother. You should be proud of your beautiful black babies. It is just that they are not meant to fish in the water like these brown birds. Now return the babies instantly. [The babies swap sides] Brown bird, as a reward for finding my daughter's ring, I shall call you the King's Fisher and I shall give you a beautiful, new, brightly coloured cloak of feathers, fit for a King.

[The King gives the brown bird the cloak of beautiful feathers].

Narrator: And so that is how the Kingfisher got it's name and beautiful feathers. Water birds are different from land birds, but each play an important part in God's beautiful world.

Prayer

Thank you God for our similarities and our differences. Help each one of us to learn the unique contribution that we can make in your world. Amen.

Hymn

No. 39 'The ink is black', in *Someone's Singing Lord*, published by A. & C. Black.

8   Animals and Birds

5–11
Assembly
Judaism

Daniel in the Lion's Den

This wonderful story lends itself to dramatization and not only this story, (in chapter 6 of the Bible) but also the whole book of Daniel makes exciting reading.

You will need the following characters:

Daniel
King Darius
First Prince
Second Prince
Third Prince
120 Princes (10 will do!)
5 Lions
Page Boy
Narrator

Narrator: (Pointing to each actor in turn, the Narrator introduces the characters to the audience and then says;) Now we are going to tell you about Daniel, a very brave man, who stood up for his belief in God.

King Darius: Come here, Daniel, I am so pleased with all your work, that I am going to put you in charge of these 120 princes here. Page boy read my proclamation.

[King puts his arm round Daniel; Page boy reads proclamation]

Page Boy: Princes, the King has ordered me to tell you, that Daniel is to be put in charge of you. You are to go to him and ask his approval before you do anything. Do you understand?

[10 princes nod, exit King and Page boy]

First Prince: Can I do this Daniel?

[Shows piece of paper, Daniel nods]

Second Prince: Will you sign this Daniel?

[Daniel signs]

Third Prince: Can I visit my Aunt?

[Daniel agrees — exit Daniel]

Narrator: The King was so pleased with everything that Daniel did for him, that he planned to put Daniel in charge of the whole kingdom. But in the meantime, the princes became very jealous that Daniel had found such favour with their King, so they put their heads together to plot against Daniel and to draw up a plan to trick him into disobeying the King.

[All the princes link arms, heads down in a sort of rugby scrum formation and move to the left]

Princes: Mutter, mutter, mutter.

[Heads up, look around, rugby scrum formation again, move to the right]

Princes: Jabber, jabber, jabber.

[Heads up, look around, rugby scrum formation again, move to the left]

Princes: Whine, whine, grumble, whine

First Prince: Right, this is what we'll do. Since we can't find anything wrong with Daniel, the only way to trick him into disobeying the king, is to make him go against his precious God. Look, he prays to his God everyday, if we make the king sign a proclamation to say that if anyone asks God or man to do anything, during the next thirty days, he will be thrown into the den of lions, then we will catch Daniel out. Come on let's go to the king and get him to sign this proclamation straight away.

[Princes go off and find the king]

Second Prince: King dear, grovel, grovel, you are so wise, and so good, and so clever; we, that is my mates and me, think that you should sign a proclamation to say that anyone who asks anything for the next thirty days of any God or man, except you, dear King, should be thrown into the lion's den. What do you say?

Third Prince: (To the audience) That will trap beloved Daniel. (To the King) Sign here dear King.

King: Well, if you insist, I will sign the paper, but I can't think why.

[Scratches his head]

Narrator: The news soon reached Daniel's ears, but Daniel knew that he would still go on praying to God. So he went straight upstairs to his bedroom and opened the windows wide and began to pray.

[Daniel kneels in prayer]

The three princes rubbed their hands together in glee. They knew that they had trapped Daniel.

First Prince: We have trapped Daniel. Come on let's go and tell the king, that someone has disobeyed his new rule.

[They hurry to find the king]

Second Prince: (To the King) Your Majesty, didn't you sign a proclamation saying that anyone who asked anything of any God, for thirty days except yourself, should be thrown into the lion's den?

King: Yes, that's right, I did.

Third Prince: Well, we know someone who has disobeyed your order. Daniel has disobeyed you, he has been up to his room, praying to his precious God. We heard him, didn't we chaps?

All the Princes: Yes, we heard him, didn't we chaps.

Narrator: When the king heard this news he was terribly upset, he beat his breast and tore his clothes and then walked up and down trying to think of some way of saving Daniel.

[King walks up and down, beating his breast and tearing his clothes, then resting his head first on one hand and then on the other]

Although the king thought and thought all day, he could not think of a way of saving Daniel. The three princes went to see the king again.

Three Princes (in unison): You have made the law, O King, therefore you must carry out the punishment.

[They rub their hands in glee]

King: O, I wish I hadn't made that silly law. I cannot save Daniel now. Send for Daniel and bring him to me.

Page Boy: Here he is, Sir.

King: I'm sorry that I have to do this Daniel, but a law is a law. Perhaps your God will save you?

Narrator: So Daniel was taken and thrown into the lions' den (lions roar, and try to scratch Daniel with their paws). The king was so upset that he spent the night without sleeping or eating or drinking. He just paced the floor, backwards and forwards, he went. As soon as it was light, the king rushed to the lion's den.

King: Are you alive Daniel? Did your God save you?

Daniel: Yes I'm alive, your Majesty. God protected me from the lions, see for yourself, I am completely unharmed.

King: Bring Daniel out of the lions' den, this instant, and today, I will make it known to all the nations that we shall serve Daniel's God, because he is the true and living God.

The Teacher needs to gather the threads together by saying something like, Daniel was very brave, to remain true to his God in the face of certain death. I wonder if we would be brave enough to stand up for what we believe in. Daniel was a very courageous man.

Prayer

Father God, we thank you for saving Daniel's life. We thank you for his example of courage and bravery. Protect each one of us. Amen.

Hymn

'He is Lord of All', in *Shalom Songs for Children from the Jewish Tradition*, translated by A. Baron

Address
'Shalom' book and cassette and price list, available from A. Baron,
6 Blenheim Gardens, Wallington,
Surrey

The Boy Who Saved a Swan

The whole class can mime this story.

You will need the following:

Characters
> Prince Siddhārtha
> Devadatta (the prince's cousin)
> Flock of Swans
> Wounded swan
> Group of Wise Men
> Group of flowers in the garden
> Narrator

Props and Costumes
> Prince's cloak
> Bow and arrow
> Swan costumes
> Red patch for wound
> Simple robes
> Flower masks

Narrator: Prince Siddhārtha was a very kind and caring boy. One day he was playing in the palace gardens.

> [Prince walks round the exotic flowers. Suitable music can be played. Flowers gently sway in the breeze]

Suddenly, a beautiful flock of swans flew over the gardens. The Prince stood and watched the beautiful birds.

> [Swans dance to suitable music]

Narrator: The Prince's cousin, Devadatta, was also playing in the palace gardens and when he saw the swans, he took his bow and arrow and shot at the birds. One graceful bird was hit and it fell at the Prince's feet.

[Swan falls at Prince's feet with an arrow stuck in it's wing and a red patch of blood staining the feathers]

Narrator: The prince tried to help the bird, but it was so frightened and shocked that it flapped its wings and hissed at the prince. But the bird could not fly. Gradually the young prince calmed the frightened bird by talking softly to it, and stroking it's head. Eventually, he was able to pull the arrow out. He ripped up a piece of his beautiful cloak and bound it around the bird's damaged wing.

Just then the prince's cousin came running over. He was shouting that as he had shot the swan, it belonged to him. He tried to pull the swan away from the prince.

[There follows a tussle with the bird first pulled one way and then the other].

Narrator: The prince, put his hand up and said 'Stop, we are only going to harm this beautiful bird, why do you want it anyway?' Devadatta said that he wanted to roast the bird at a huge party that he was having for his friends.

[He mimes the action]

The prince sadly shook his head and said that he only wanted to care for the swan and make it better and strong enough to return it to the flock. The prince said, 'let us go to the wise men and ask them to settle our quarrel'.

[Enter group of wise men, who sit cross-legged on the floor]

Narrator: The two boys carried the swan to the wise men and asked them who should keep the swan. For a long time, the wise men put their heads together to decide to whom the swan should be given. Then the oldest wise man stood up, and pointing to Prince Siddhārtha, he said that the swan should be given to the Prince, because the Prince had tried to save the swan's life. Whereas, the Prince's cousin, Devadatta, had tried to take it's life away.

The Prince joyfully took the beautiful bird away. He stroked it and fed it and talked to it and eventually the swan was strong enough and well enough to fly back to the flock. Devadatta was left scowling and angry and he stamped his feet in rage.

Prayer

Father God, may we never harm birds, or be cruel to animals. Amen

Hymn

No. 42 'I love God's tiny creatures', *in Someone's Singing Lord*, published by A. & C. Black.

**5–11
Assembly
Sikhism**

The Donkey in Lion's Clothing

This is the story that Guru Gobind Singh told, in order to show his Sikh followers, how important it was to have a uniform that was respected. He told the story in 1699 when the brotherhood or Khalsa was first formed (see also pages 53–55).

You will need the following:

Characters
Donkey
Donkey's master
Master's friend
Cockerel
Pig
Dog
Cat
6 townspeople
Tiger
Monkeys at water-hole
Birds
Tree

Props/Costumes
Donkey ears, tail
Master's stick
Lion skin and mask
Cockerel mask
Pig mask
Dog mask
Cat mask
6 robes
Tiger mask
Monkey masks
Bird masks
Tree costume

The whole class can be involved in the mime. The teacher, or one of the older children, could act as a narrator.

Narrator: Once upon a time, there was a donkey with big ears and a long tail.

[Donkey comes to the front of the hall and shows his big ears and tail]

Narrator: He was a very lazy animal, and he would much rather eat, than work. The Donkey's master had to prod him to get him to move or to carry his baskets to market for him.

[Master prods donkey with a stick, the donkey refuses to move; the master prods the donkey again; the donkey brays and moves one step. The action is repeated a few times]

Narrator: One fine day, the master went to visit his friend. The friend showed the master the head and skin of a lion that had been shot by some poachers. [Mime the action] Whilst the two friends were talking, the donkey started to sniff around for a bucket of food, when suddenly the lion's head and skin fell on the donkey's head.

[Donkey ears are exchanged for the lion mask]

Narrator: The friend and the master were so busy talking that they had not seen what had happened and when they turned round, all they saw, or thought they saw, was a lion. They ran away in fright.

[Mime the action]

Narrator: A cockerel was pecking some corn when he looked up and he too, thought he saw a lion, so he flew off squawking and flapping his wings.

[Mime the action]

Narrator: A pig was scratching about for food when it backed into the donkey wearing the lion skin. It gave one enormous squeal and rushed out of the yard.

[Mime the action]

Narrator: A dog was chewing a bone and had not seen the kefuffle going on, until the donkey ambled up to smell the bone, to see if he would like to nibble it. The dog was so frightened that it could not bark and ran off with its tail between it's legs.

[Mime the action]

Narrator: A cat was sitting in the sun licking it's paws and washing behind it's ears, when suddenly she saw the lion's shadow in front of her. She gave one long miouw and ran away.

[Mime the action]

Narrator: The donkey could not think why everyone was running away from him, but he did not really care, as long as they had left him some food, he would eat it all up.

[Donkey eats the food]

Narrator: By and by, the donkey began to get bored in the yard and decided to go off to town to see what food he could find there. He was most surprised when he met a group of townspeople and they all ran off in different directions, screaming.

[Townsfolk mime the actions]

Narrator: The donkey wandered back through the jungle, when suddenly he came across a tiger. The donkey was very afraid because he was certain that the tiger would chase him, but to his utmost surprise, the tiger took one look at him and disappeared.

[Mime the actions]

Narrator: The donkey made his way to the water-hole, where a group of monkeys were having a drink. They were chittering and chattering and at first they did not notice the donkey, until one monkey pointed and all the other monkeys clutched each other in fright, and made a fearful, terrified racket, before leaping off into the trees.

[Monkeys mime the action and noise]

Narrator: Poor old donkey had no idea why everyone was running away from him. As it was near dusk he came across some peaceful birds all roosting and trying to go to sleep. But when they saw the donkey in the lion's skin, they woke up and squawked and flew off in all directions.

[Birds fly all round the hall in and out of the seated children, squawking, before coming to rest]

Narrator: The donkey went to sleep and in the morning he decided to go and find his master, as he was very hungry by this time. [Enter master] As soon as he saw his master, he started to bray loudly, 'hee-haw, hee-haw' he said. The master was just about to run away when it occurred to him that it was very strange for a lion to bray like his donkey. [Master stands and stares] In his rush to get to his master, the donkey's headdress and skin got caught up in a thorn tree; it was whisked off the donkey's back and he became a donkey once more. [Mime the action] At once, the master recognised the donkey and took out his stick and gave him a prod.

End the drama, by explaining that, all the time, the donkey was wearing the lion's head and skin, everyone was afraid of him. Guru Gobind Singh told this story to his followers in order to show them, that all the time that they wore their uniforms, people would show them respect.

Prayer

Heavenly Father, help each one of us to respect each other, whatever our race or colour or creed. Amen.

Hymn

No. 30 'You'll sing a song and I'll sing a song' in *Tinder-box: 66 Songs for Children*, published by A. & C. Black.

5–11
Assembly
Islam

The Thirsty Dog
(An Islamic Tale)

(Adaptation of 'A Thirsty Dog' in *Love all Creatures* published by The Islamic Foundation, Leicester and reproduced with their permission)

Many years ago, a man called Hasan, felt that it was time for him to make his pilgrimage to Makkah. He lived in a tiny village near Medina. The journey to Makkah would be very long and arduous. Being a poor man, he could not afford the camel transport to Makkah, so he decided to walk. He took with him, a white robe, sandals, a skin containing water and enough bread for the first two or three days of the nine-day journey. He thought that he could stop on the way to buy more food and to ask for more water at the Bedouin camps that he would pass on the rest of the journey.

All went well for the first few days. He stopped and chatted to people on his way. He told them that he was making his Hajj or pilgrimage to Makkah, and the people always gave him water to drink and once or twice he was invited to share an evening meal with a family on the route. He slept under the stars, only wrapping his cloak tightly around him as the heat of the days turned into cool nights.

Soon he left the towns and villages behind him and he knew that he must cross a huge desert before he reached Makkah. He made sure that he had enough water in his water skin and enough food to make this perilous part of the journey. He had with him, his very own astrolabe or compass, that had been given to his family many years before, and had been passed down from father to son, over the generations. With this instrument, he could navigate his way by the stars. The astrolabe had been invented by very clever Muslim scientists many centuries earlier.

As the desert was so hot, he thought that it would be better to travel by night and rest during the day. Once again, all went well for the first two or three days and nights, when suddenly, Hasan realized that he was running out of water. He decided to use the water very sparingly, to make sure that it lasted until he reached the next camp. But even so, his throat began to get parched and his lips began to crack and he saw no signs of civilization ahead. Hasan began to feel desperate. He looked this way and that. All he could see was sand; miles and miles of dusty sand, stretching in every direction. Hasan began to feel very weak and tired now. He drained the last drops of water from the skin, and stumbled on, afraid that he would surely die.

Fearing that the end was near, he stumbled against a clump of rocks. As he sank to his knees, Hasan's hand touched something round and hard. This was no ordinary rock, it was something man-made, certainly. The stones had been hewn and placed in a circular pattern. Frantically, Hasan brushed away the sand with his bare hands, and, sure enough, there was a round circle of stones, underneath the sand. Over the top of the circle, lay a heavy stone. Heaving this aside, with all the energy that he could muster, Hasan discovered a deep, dark cavern. Could this hold water? And even if it did, how could he get down to it? He quickly looked about him to see if he could find a small pebble that he could drop into the depths, to listen for the 'plopping' sound, that would tell him that the stone was hitting water. To his great relief, he did not have to search for long. There beside the circular stones was a chipping left by the men, who had hewn out the rock. Very carefully, and very gingerly, he leant over the edge and dropped the stone. For a few seconds, he heard absolutely nothing; nothing but silence. Then to his great joy, somewhere, deeply below him, within the tubular hole, he heard a tiny splash. WATER. He nearly danced for joy, until he realized with utter dismay, that he had no way of getting the water up. He did not have a rope on which to let down his water skin, or on which he could lower himself down to the water. The life-saving drink was utterly useless to him. He was within reach of water and yet he was going to die of thirst.

He lay back in the sands; too tired to move, too tired to think. Yet as he lay there, he slowly knew what he was going to do. If he was going to die anywhere, why not die, trying to reach the water, rather than in this baking sun?

He heaved himself over the side of the well and to his amazement, he found a foothold for his right foot. Letting himself down gently, a bit further, he found another small crevice for his left foot. But he was still hanging on to the circular top with his hands. What on earth was he going to do, when he had to let go of the top? Cautiously, he eased himself down a bit further, and gripped the stones above his head as he went. He managed to hang on to the rough rock above him, whilst he searched first with one foot for a crevice and then with the other foot. Inch by inch, he eased himself slowly downwards. It was a tiring and exhausting journey and he was not at all sure that he would make it, let alone have the energy to get back up again. Miraculously, after a very long time in the dark, dank tunnel, his toes touched something cold and wet. Gingerly, he poked his toe a little bit further down, and found that he had reached the water. Easing himself down still further, he let go with one hand and managed to swing his water skin into the water. Sadly, he could not obtain much water in this way, but he was afraid that if he went down any further into the water, he would slip. Very slowly, he pulled the skin up to his lips and drank the pure, clean water. Precariously balanced as he was, he repeated this action several times, until his thirst was quenched. Finally, he made his ascent, once again, up the perilous rocks.

Slowly, slowly he pulled himself up, until at last his fingertips reached the curved stones and he was able to pull himself out of the well. He lay there on the sand panting with exhaustion and drained the last drop of water from the skin. He knew that he must re-start his journey, now that he had quenched his thirst, and find the nearest camp for food. Just as he pulled himself to his feet, a dog appeared out of nowhere. Hasan could see instantly that the dog was exhausted and as thirsty, and as near to death, as he had been. What on earth could he do to help the poor animal? He had drained the last drop of water from his water skin, and he certainly could not make that perilous journey down the well again.

As Hasan looked at the dog, the dog whimpered and licked Hasan, and looked up at him with big, sad, trusting eyes. 'Oh no', thought Hasan, 'don't look at me like that. I really can't help you'. The dog whimpered again and licked Hasan's hand, this time the dog fell over, as he was so weak and lay dying in the sand.

'Hold on', croaked Hasan 'I'll save you if I can'. Without thinking about his own safety, Hasan went down the well a second time. He slipped several times, cutting his fingers and feet in his efforts to cling onto the sides of the well. But in the end he made it back up to the top with a small skin full of the reviving water. Gently he dripped the water on to the dog's parched tongue. Slowly, slowly the dog revived and sat up. But it was now dark. Hasan felt in his pockets for his astrolabe to guide him out of the desert. To his dismay, it had gone. It must have fallen into the water when he had slipped on that perilous second journey. Once again Hasan knew that he was facing death. Without his compass, he would be completely lost, destined to die in the sand.

Puzzled by a tug on his robe, he looked down to see the dog, trying to pull him to a place beyond the rocks. 'Stop it, silly dog', Hasan admonished the animal, 'Aren't we in enough trouble without you ripping my robe by pulling me over these rocks?' But the dog insisted and kept pulling Hasan's robe. Then the dog ran ahead, and only stopped to look behind him to see if Hasan was following him. When Hasan stood in puzzlement, the dog ran back and gave Hasan a further tug as though he wanted Hasan to follow.

It was pitch black and Hasan stumbled after the dog for what seemed like hours. Sudddenly, as the sun began to rise, Hasan saw beyond him the unmistakable shapes of dwellings, and a dog barking for joy.

Prayer

Almighty God, may we always be kind to all animals. Amen

9 Leaders

5–11
Assembly
Judaism

Abraham's Story

Abraham's story is very important to Jews, Christians and Muslims alike. The story can be read in the Torah, or in the Bible, Genesis, chapters 12–25, or in the Qu'ran.

To the Jews, Abraham, is seen as the father of the Jewish people. A righteous man, who taught that there was only one God. The Torah tells of the convenant that God made with Abraham and how God would make him the father of a very great nation, and that all his descendants would become God's 'chosen people'. God would give them their own special land, if Abraham obeyed and went where God would lead him.

The story can be told, just as it was, or it can be acted out (see following pages). Emphasise the facts that Abraham (then called Abram) and Sarah, (then called Sarai) were very courageous to set out on an unknown path, simply trusting God and leaving a very comfortable life in the City of Ur, to start a new life in an unknown land, that God would show them. They had to leave behind them, family and friends, and even then, Sarah was quite old and childless.

The class should understand how worried Sarah must have felt when she did not have the promised baby straight away. They should also understand something of the significance of the three visitors to Abraham and Sarah's tent in the land of Canaan and finally, understand the joy when the baby eventually arrived. The baby was called Isaac. One of Abraham's grandchildren was later called Jacob or Israel and he, in turn, had twelve sons who became the fathers of the twelve tribes of Israel.

The children can act out the story as the teacher reads from the book.

You will need the following characters:

God
Moon God
Abraham
Sarah
Crowd
Servants
Friends
3 Visitors
Baby

The main elements of the story are these:

1   The people are all worshipping Moon Gods.
    [Crowd bows down before Moon God]
2   God speaks to Abraham and promises that if Abraham will go where God leads him, God will make him the father of a very great nation.
    [Mime the actions]
3   So Abraham sets off with his servants.
    [Abraham, Sarah and servants trudge round the hall several times. They can weave in and out of the children, looking for a place to rest. The teacher can ad lib the actions]
4   Friends laugh at Abraham, for not knowing where he will eventually settle down.
    [Friends mime the action]
5   Many years passed, at last they reached the land of Canaan. Abraham and Sarah were getting very old and Sarah was very upset that she still did not have the promised baby.
    [Sarah mimes her weeping to Abraham]
6   Then three men appear at Abraham's tent door. Abraham kills the best calf and Sarah bakes some cakes. They give the visitors the food.
    [Characters mime these actions]
7   One of the visitors tells Abraham, that by this time next year, Sarah will have a son. Sarah, who is listening at the tent door laughs, because she does not believe him.
    [The characters mime the actions]
8   Abraham knows that this is God speaking, so when the visitors depart, Abraham and Sarah hug each other with joy.
    [Action is mimed]
9   Finally the baby arrives, they call him Isaac. Sarah and Abraham invite all their friends to a special celebration.
    [Friends dance and have a party. The baby is shown to all the people]

Prayer

Almighty God, we thank you, that you chose Abraham to be the father of a very great nation. Amen.

Hymn

'Oz V'Shalom'
Psalm 29 verse 11 (See tune below)
Adonai oz l'amo yiteyn
Adonai oz l'amo yiteyn
Adonai y'vareh et amo b'shalom
Adonai y'vareh et amo b'shalom

The Lord will give strength to his people
The Lord will bless his people with peace

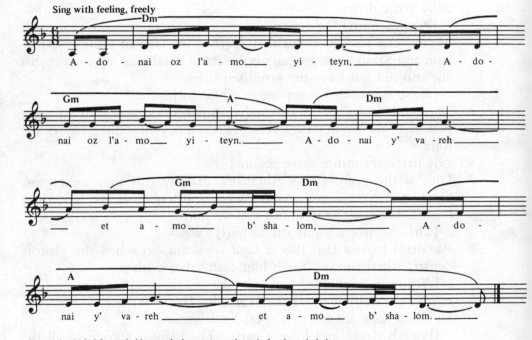

Singers should feel free to hold on to the long notes at the end of each musical phrase.

or

'Adon Olam' in *Sephardic Songs of Praise*, by Abraham Lopes Cardozo published by Tara Publications, Cedarhurst, N.Y.
This can be sung to the tune of Clementine or Walsing Matilda (see tune overleaf.).

Adon Olam

Adon olam is often sung at the end of morning services on Shabbat or a festival. It has a regular, common metre and fits many existing tunes though Jewish composers have written umpteen melodies specially for it (A.W.).

Adon olam asher malah b'terem kol y'tzir nivra (Adon olam),
l'eyt na'asah k'hevtzo kol azai meleh sh'mo nikra (Adon olam).

V'aharei kihlot hakol, l'va'ado yimloh nora (Adon olam),
V'hu haya v'hu hove, v'hu yiy'yeh b'tifarah (Adon olam).

V'hu ehad v'eyn sheyni, l'hamshiylo l'hahbirah (Adon olam),
B'li reshit, b'li tahlit, v'lo haoz v'hamisrah (Adon olam).

V'hu eyli v'hai goali, v'tzur hevli b'yom tzarah (Adon olam),
V'hu nisi umanusi, m'nat kosi b'yom ekra (Adon olam).

B'yado afkid ruhi, beyt ishan v'a'ira (Adon olam),
V'im ruhi g'viati, adonai li v'lo ira (Adon olam).

Eternal Lord who ruled alone
before creation of all forms,
when all was made at His desire
then as the king was He revealed.

And after everything shall end
alone, in wonder, will He reign,
as once He was, so is He now,
the glory that will never change.

He is the One, no other is
to be compared, to stand beside,
neither before, nor following,
His is the strength and His the might.

This is my God, my life He saves,
the rock I grasp in deep despair,
the flag I wave, the place I hide,
He shares my cup the day I call.

Within his hand I lay my soul
both when I sleep and when I wake,
and with my soul my body too,
my Lord is close I shall not fear.

This English translation fits the same metre.

Muhammad
('Peace be upon Him')

It is very important to remember that whenever Muhammad's name is mentioned, Muslims pay respect to his name by saying the words 'Peace be upon Him'. And because Muslims believe that Muhammad was God's messenger, it is inappropriate for children to draw pictures of Muhammad or to act out the story of his life. Therefore, this assembly takes the form of a quiet, reflective description of Muhammad's birth, life and death.

Muhammad was born in AD 570 in the Arabian City of Makkah. His mother's name was Aminah, and his father's name was Abd Allah. Unfortunately, Muhammad's father died before he was born and his mother died when he was only six. So he was brought up firstly, by his grandfather, Abd al-Muttalib, until his death two years later, and then by his Uncle, Abu Talib.

Muhammad spent the years of his youth tending his uncle's sheep and goats and working with the trading caravans. He became known for his honesty and trustworthiness. He later married Khadijah, his employer, and they had six children.

Muhammad was shocked by life in the city of Makkah. He saw the people worshipping stone idols, drinking and fighting. He believed in one God, and so saddened was he, by what he saw, that it became his custom to go away alone to the hills and pray to Allah (God).

One night, when he was about 40 years old, alone in a cave on Mount Hira, the Angel Jibra'il appeared to him, with words written on a piece of cloth. The angel told Muhammad to repeat the words that he spoke to him, but alas, Muhammad could not repeat the words. Three times the angel told Muhammad to recite the words, then Jibra'il embraced him and this time he was able to repeat the words. Later these words were written down and they became part of the Qur'an, the Holy Book of the Muslim people. Further revelations continued for the next twenty-three years, and every word was written down.

The name Islam, was given to this new teaching. Allah revealed to Muhammad, that Allah was the one true God who created the heavens and the earth and everything that lives on the earth. Allah told Muhammad that idols were not to be worshipped, and that if people continued to live corrupt lives, they would be punished.

Muhammad started to tell the people of Makkah this, but they would not listen to him and plotted to kill him. Muhammad managed to escape with the help of his young cousin Ali, who exchanged places with Muhammad and lay in his bed. There is a story that a spider and a bird also helped Muhammad to escape from his enemies. Muhammad was hiding in a cave on Mount Thawr. The spider spun a web and the bird built it's nest over the mouth of the cave, so that when the enemies passed by they thought that the cave had not been disturbed for many years and so did not go inside.

Muhammad eventually reached the city of al-Madinah. The journey from Makkah to al-Madinah is very important to Muslims, it is called the Hijrah.

It was in al-Madinah, that the first mosque was built. The Muslims prayed five times each day and they learnt that they should follow God's law, treat one another with respect and give some of their money to the poor.

After many fierce battles, even the people in Makkah believed the message of Islam. Muhammad died when he was sixty-three.

At the end of the story, give the children time to think about some of the things that Muhammad taught i.e. that there was only one God, who is the creator of heaven and earth; that the people were not to worship man-made idols, and that all mankind should treat each other with respect.

Mahatma Gandhi

The life story of Mahatma Gandhi, can either be re-told in an assembly, or the events of his life can be dramatized for the whole school to watch.

The following account covers the main events in his life. Mohandas Karamchand Gandhi was born into a Hindu family in 1869. He grew up learning to speak his native language, Gujarati and following the Hindu religion, devoted to God in the form of Vishnu the Preserver of the universe, which believes in a loving relationship between God and humanity (A. Constant, *Man of Peace, The Story of Mahatma Gandhi*, RMEP, 1985).

Like other Hindu families, Mohandas' parents believed in arranging their children's marriages, and so when Mohandas was only thirteen, his parents arranged for him to marry Kasturbai, who was also only thirteen. However, Mohandas continued with his studies, as Kasturbai often returned to her parents home for long periods.

When Mohandas was nearly nineteen years of age, he left Kasturbai and their young son in India and went to study law in England.

It was whilst he was in London, that he read one of the books which many Hindus regard as sacred, the Bhagavad Gita. He also studied the Bible. Both these holy books made a deep impression on Gandhi that was to influence the rest of his life.

As soon as he had passed his law examinations, Gandhi returned to India. He was offered a chance to work in South Africa. So, grasping the opportunity with both hands, he left Kasturbai and his two sons and set off for Pretoria. It was whilst he was on the train to Pretoria, that something happened that was to change the whole of his life. He was sitting in a first class compartment, as he had a first class train ticket, when he encountered racial discrimination for the very first time. Because of his colour, he was ordered to sit in a third class compartment, and when he refused, he was ordered to get off the train. Poor Gandhi, spent all night on the railway station platform, feeling miserable, cold and hungry. It was this experience that lead him to fight against racial injustice and prejudice; not with weapons, but with peaceful methods.

'He invented a name for the two weapons he would use: *Satyagraha* (holding on to truth), which meant standing up for something you were convinced was right, and *ahimsa*, meaning love operating through non-violence' (Audrey Constant, *Man of Peace, the Story of Mahatma Gandhi*, RMEP, 1985. page 10).

Gandhi sent for his family, and over the next twenty years, he became a prominent leader of the Indian people, setting up a newspaper telling the world about the racial injustice in South Africa and using non–violent means to get racial laws abolished. He was imprisoned many times during this period. From 1899–1902 there was the Boer War, between Britain and the South African Boers, and Gandhi, feeling that he should support the British, organised the Indian Ambulance Corps for which he was later awarded a medal by the British Empire.

In 1915, Gandhi returned to his native India. He travelled around the country assessing the needs of the people. He knew that the people needed a proper education and that they could only be self-sufficient if they developed their own industries. So he started spinning cloth using a simple spinning wheel and insisted that his followers learnt to spin and so boycott the importation of foreign cloth.

At this time, he founded a religious community outside the city of Ahmdabad, and he tried to teach the people that treating people as 'untouchable' was as unjust as the racial discrimination that he had encountered in South Africa. He taught the people that the untouchables were all God's children and therefore welcome in his community and temples. It was at this time that one of India's greatest poets, Rabindranath Tagore, called Gandhi 'Mahatma' (Great Soul).

An example of his 'greatness' is illustrated by the way he settled land rent disputes. First, he sought justice from the Government and when they refused to comply, he organised the farm workers to go on strike. He ordered the strikers not to use violence of any sort, and if they were beaten, they were not to fight back. At last, the government listened to Gandhi and ordered the landlords to repay the high rents back to the workers.

After the war in 1918, Gandhi hoped that the British would consider Home Rule for India. But instead, Britain passed new and harsher laws against India ruling its own country. As a result, Gandhi ordered a one-day national strike, but some of the strikers forgot Gandhi's rule of non-violence and some people were killed and many were injured. Gandhi was so horrified, that he went on an extended fast.

The British were now afraid that there would be an open revolt in the country and so they called in the troops. This was how they made the most terrible mistake. It was a Holy day for Sikhs on 12th April 1919, and many women and children were gathered together in their Holy City at Amritsar, when the British troops opened fire on the unarmed festival goers. Approximately 400 innocent people were massacred. Gandhi never forgot this terrible event and held a twenty-four hour fast every year afterwards in memory of the massacre at Amritsar.

It was after this, that Gandhi, now leader of the Indian National Congress, ordered the people to support a programme of 'non-violent civil disobedience' (Constant). Goods were boycotted and taxes were not paid. He was imprisoned by the British Government for his action. Two years later he was released and he fasted in protest against the growing conflict between Hindus and Muslims; only calling off his fast, when the leaders of both communities urged their people to try and live peaceably together.

Gandhi and the Indian National Congress still wanted independence. A law had been passed forbidding Indians to make their own salt. So in 1930, in order to bring their plight to the attention of the world press, Gandhi set out on a march to the sea, to collect and make salt. He was joined by thousands of protestors. The march took twenty-four days to complete, gathering world attention as it did so. Gandhi was imprisoned yet again and he was only released in order to take part in a conference about India's future in London in 1931. But the British Government still refused to give India Home Rule and imposed an even stricter regime. Once again, Gandhi and many thousands of supporters, were imprisoned.

It was only after the Second World War, that the question of Home Rule was finally considered. But once again the path to progress was not smooth.

The Muslims wanted their own state to be called Pakistan, under their own leader, Ali Jinnah. Gandhi did not want to see India divided. The result was terrible fighting between Muslims and Hindus with many killed and injured.

Lord Mountbatten became the last British Viceroy of India in 1947. Seeing no way to have a united India, the Indian Congress, agreed to giving the Muslim leader, Jinnah a separate state to be called Pakistan. And so it was, that on 15th August 1947, India and Pakistan finally celebrated their independence. But Gandhi could not join in the celebration as he could foresee that it would cause a deep rift between the people. Fierce fighting broke out again, and once again, Gandhi fasted until Hindu and Muslim leaders promised that there would be no more fighting.

It was on 30th January 1948 that Mahatma Gandhi was killed by a Hindu priest, who believed that Hindus had suffered because Gandhi had tried to unite Hindus and Muslims.

It was a tragic end for a man who had only sought to right wrongs by peaceful means.

Prayer

Heavenly Father, this great man of peace gave us an example to follow and yet still, there is fighting all over the world. May we work together for peace, and may it start right here with us, your children. Amen.

Hymn

No. 147 'Make me a channel of your peace', in *Come and Praise 2*, published by BBC, London, 1988.

Siddhārtha Gautama

Siddhārtha Gautama became the Buddha some six hundred years before the birth of Christ. Buddhists do not believe the Buddha was a God, but they do revere his teaching.

To act out the story of his life, you will need the following characters:

> King
> Queen
> Prince Siddhārtha
> 2 Wise Men
> Yashodharā (Siddhārtha's wife)
> Old Man
> Sick Man
> Dead Man and group of Mourners
> First Holy Man
> Servant
> 5 Holy Men
> Followers
> Narrator

Narrator: One upon a time there lived a King and Queen in Northern India. They had a young son called Prince Siddhārtha. He was a lovely boy in every way and the King and Queen loved him very much. One day, when he was still quite young, two wise men came to see the King and Queen.

Wise Men: Your Majesty, let us see your son.

> [Siddhārtha is brought before the wise men]

First Wise Man: Your Majesty, we believe that your son will grow up to be a very great leader.

Second Wise Man: We think that he will give up all this wealth and leave the palace forever to teach others how to find peace and happiness.

> [Exit wise men]

Narrator: Now the King and Queen were extremely upset when they heard this, and so they decided there and then to protect their son from all unhappiness, so that he would never have to leave home to teach others how to find happiness. They surrounded him with beautiful flowers, and gardens and friends in the palace and they never let him leave the palace walls to see the suffering outside. When he grew up, they found a wife for Siddhārtha, a young cousin called Yashodharā.

[Yashodharā puts a wedding veil on and the pair walk around the hall]

But one day, Siddhārtha was alone with his servant, he began to question his servant about the world outside.

Siddhārtha: Please tell me what it is like outside these palace walls ?

Servant: I cannot tell you, master, I have been forbidden to talk about the world outside.

Siddhārtha: Then if you will not tell me, show me.

Servant: Oh master, we will get into very serious trouble if I take you outside.

Siddhārtha: Look, I will take all the blame, come on, let's just have a little walk outside these walls.

Narrator: Reluctantly, the servant took the prince outside, but the prince met four people who changed his life forever. The first person he met, was an old man.

Old Man: Good day, young Sir.

Siddhārtha: Good day. Tell me sir, why do you hobble and walk with a bent back, and why are you so thin, and your skin is so wrinkled?

Old Man: It is because I am very, very old. Have you never seen an old person before? We must all grow old, you know.

Narrator: Siddhārtha was horrified, he shook his head and held his hands up in horror. Next, the young prince heard someone groaning and saw before him a very sick man.

Siddhārtha: Oh, what is wrong with you? Why are you moaning?

Sick Man: I am very ill, young sir, and I am in dreadful pain. There is no cure for my sickness, oh please help me.

Siddhārtha: I don't know how to help you, how I wish I could. I have never seen a sick person before.

Narrator: No sooner had the prince spoken to the sick man, than he heard a group of people crying. He looked around to see where the noise was coming from and saw a dead man for the very first time.

Siddhārtha: Oh tell me, tell me, why are you all crying.

Mourners: We are crying because our dear friend is dead.

Siddhārtha: What does dead mean?

Mourner: It means that we will not see him any more. He will no longer sit and eat or drink with us. We are crying because we shall miss him very much.

Narrator: The prince shook his head and sadly walked on, he had never seen so much suffering as he had seen that day. The prince met one more person and these four encounters changed his life forever. The fourth person was a Holy man.

Siddhārtha: Oh sir, you look so calm and peaceful, tell me what is the secret of your happiness ?

Holy Man: Young man, you must learn this for yourself, by searching out the great truths about living and learn to understand why there is suffering and evil in this world.

Narrator: Without another word, Siddhārtha hurried back to the palace and kissed his sleeping wife and baby goodbye. He took off his princely robes and put on a rough cloak and set off to find the meaning of what he had seen. He found five Holy men, who taught him many things. They ate very little and life was very hard.

[The five Holy men sit in a circle with the prince and mime discussion]

However, Siddhārtha did not think that they had all the answers. Neither living such a hard life, nor living in such luxury as he had lived in the palace, was the answer to finding happiness. So he left the five Holy men and went away by himself, until he found a large tree. He sat underneath this tree and started to eat a little food and when he felt better, he started to think deeply about the questions that were puzzling him. After thinking for a very long time, Siddhārtha suddenly realized that pain and suffering were a part of life which we all have to accept. It was no use getting angry or upset about it. Old age and death too, are a part of life, to which we have to come to terms.

Siddhārtha felt that much unhappiness was caused by people's greed and selfishness. So he set out to tell others about what he had learnt, and what he called his Middle Way. It was then that he became known as the Buddha or 'Enlightened One'.

[The scene ends with the Buddha teaching the followers, the things that he had learnt]

Prayer

Father God, help us to accept the sad things as well as the good things. Save us from being greedy or selfish. Amen.

Hymn

No. 102 'You can't stop rain from falling down', in *Come and Praise 2*, published by BBC, London, 1988.

Guru Nanak

The birth of Sikhism as a religion, begins with the birth of Guru Nanak, as a teacher. Guru means teacher or holy man, but Guru Nanak's actual ministry only began, when he was about thirty years old.

As mentioned on pages 53 and 89, some Sikhs object to their Guru being portrayed in drama and so it is proper to check with the local Sikh community before acting the following play. If it proves unacceptable, the part of Nanak, should be simply retold by the story-teller.

Guru Nanak's life story is a lovely narrative, about a man born to lead his people in a new way. He was, in fact, born into a Hindu family, the son of Mehta Kalu, a rich business man. He was born in Northern India, in the Punjab, which is now part of Pakistan, and was then ruled by the Muslims. Both of these two religions had a great influence on him. But Guru Nanak was to teach that there was neither Hindu nor Muslim and that rituals did not make a person holy but following God was the only way.

The following playlet is a story from his childhood. *You will need the following characters*:

Nanak
Mehta Kalu, Nanak's father
Bala, Nanak's friend
Villagers
Holy Men
Narrator

Mehta Kalu: Nanak my son, come here. I want you to grow up into a fine business man like me. I am going to give you twenty rupees, so that you can buy as many different things as possible from the nearby villages and then return here to Talwandi and sell the items at a profit. That's how we make our money in business you know.

Nanak: Yes father. I will do as you say, but father, I do not want to become a business man like you. I am more interested in finding out about God. But of course, I will try to please you.

Mehta Kalu: You must learn my trade my son, or else how are you to become successful like me ?

Nanak: I will try father. Can I take my friend Bala along with me?

Mehta Kalu: Yes, of course you can, now off you go. Buy lots of things to bring back and sell.

Narrator: The two boys set off, and went from village to village searching for things to buy, but not seeing anything they particularly wanted, they decided to move on to one of the larger towns.

[The boys mime visiting the villagers, who shake their heads and hold up empty hands]

Suddenly, the boys came across a group of Holy men who were very hungry.

[The Holy men hold out empty begging bowls]

You see, the Holy men had given away all their possessions, in order to give their lives to God, and they depended on the generosity of the people that they met, to give them food or money. Without a seconds hesitation, Nanak took out his money and gave it all to the Holy men.

Nanak: I can see that you are very hungry. I am sure my father will understand if I give you all our money, so that you can buy some food. You seem so hungry. Here you are, please take it. Take it all.

Holy Men: (In unison) Thank you, thank you, young man. You will be greatly blessed because of your generosity to us.

Bala: Oh Nanak, how could you give away all the money? Your father will be furious with you. We were supposed to spend the money on buying goods to sell at home. Oh Nanak, whatever shall we do now ?

Nanak: We shall go straight home and tell my father exactly what I have done. I am sure my father would have done the same thing in my place. Giving money to starving men is much more important than buying things. Of course he will understand. Come along.

Narrator: So the two boys set off for the long walk home. Nanak's father saw them from a long way off and went out to greet them.

Mehta Kalu: Back so soon, where are the goods you have bought with all my money?

Nanak: Oh father, I know you will understand, I have given all the money away to some starving holy men, so that they can buy food.

Mehta Kalu: You did what? You wicked boy. Money doesn't grow on trees you know, you will be soundly beaten for your disobedience.

Narrator: Poor Nanak was scolded severely for his kindness, but even as a young boy, he cared more about people than about things. He grew up to love God greatly and when he was about thirty years old, he went away for three days, and on his return he told his friends that he had had a vision of God. He felt that God had told him that being a Hindu or a Muslim was not as important as living holy lives. Guru Nanak travelled the country telling the people to love God and their fellow men. He told the people that all men were equal in God's sight. So that the people would remember his words, Guru Nanak put his message in songs or hymns.

Later these hymns came to be written down and became known as the Mool Mantra or Perfect words, which today, are a part of the Sikhs' Holy book, the Guru Granth Sahib.

Prayer

Father God, help us to love you and one another. Help us to live in peace and harmony with all people. Amen.

Hymn

No. 146 'We ask that we live and we labour in peace, in peace', in *Come and Praise 2*, published by BBC, London, 1988.

10   Some Further Background Information for the Teachers' Reference

Judaism

Background Information

Torah

The Holy writings of the Jews (which also make up the first five books of the Christian Bible). 'Jews believe that the five books of the Torah contain the words that God spoke to Moses on the Mount Sinai about 3,400 years ago'. (Sarah Thorley)

Talmud

The Talmud provides a detailed explanation of the Torah

Abraham

He lived approximately 4,000 years ago. He taught the people that there was only one God, before that, the people had worshipped many Gods.

The Covenant

The Torah tells how God made a covenant with Abraham. God promised that Abraham and his descendants would be God's 'Chosen people', but this would place a responsibility on them to work for Him. He would lead them to a new land and He would be their God. Abraham's descendants became the twelve tribes of Israel, the Israelites.

Moses

About 400 years after the death of Abraham, the Israelites were made slaves in Egypt. Moses lead the Israelites out of Egypt. Read the exciting story of the Parting of the Red Sea in Exodus Chapter 14. Later, God gave Moses the Ten Commandments and other Laws about how the Israelites should live their lives. This is in the Torah. (You can also read it in the Bible, Exodus, chapter 20.)

Hebrew

This was the language that was spoken by the early Jews and is spoken in Israel today.

Aron Hakodesh, the Holy Ark

The Torah scrolls are kept in the Ark, usually in the east end of every synagogue, facing towards Jerusalem. (N.B. it is only in the east end in western societies!)

Shabbat or Sabbath

The day of rest for the Jewish people. (See next section).

Menorah

This is the seven branched candlestick. Reference to the candlestick can be found in Exodus, chapter 25, verses 31–37. This is the official emblem of the state of Israel.

JEWISH FAMILY LIFE

Background Information

Naming Ceremony

Boys and girls are sometimes given a secular name as well as a Hebrew name and a blessing at the synagogue on the Shabbat (or Sabbath) after his/her birth. There is a special circumcision ceremony for a boy, eight days after he is born. (Read Genesis, chapter 17, verses 10–14 for the special covenant made between God and Abraham regarding this ceremony.)

Bar/Bat Mitzvah

There is a special Bar Mitzvah ceremony for boys at about the age of thirteen. Girls become Bat Mitzvah at twelve years of age. Bar Mitzvah means 'Son of the Commandment', Bat Mitzvah means 'Daughter of the Commandment'. The child becomes responsible for himself/herself and for observing the Jewish Law. He/she passes from childhood to adulthood. Until Bar/Bat Mitzvah, the child's parents would be responsible for the child's deeds. Now the child is considered old enough to judge right from wrong. Before Bar/Bat Mitzvah the child will have studied hard under the guidance of a Rabbi or teacher. Now he/she will be called to read the Torah in front of everyone at the synagogue. (See assembly on pages 103–104)

Shabbat or Sabbath

Shabbat is observed from sunset on Friday night to sunset on Saturday night. No work is done during this time. Three special meals are prepared, and the Sabbath candles are lit on the Friday night by the mother of the family, who says the Shabbat prayer over the candles.

Kiddush

The father recites a blessing or Kiddush over the wine at these special meals.

Hallot

These are two special twisted loaves of bread. There are two, as a reminder of the double portion of manna, which God gave to the Jews each Sabbath when they were wandering in the wilderness.

Hannukiyah

Nine branched candlestick used in synagogues and Jewish homes during the festival of Hannukah.

Shalom

A greeting of peace, each member of the family greets each other and friends with this distinctive word.

Synagogue

This is the Jewish place for study, meeting and prayer. The main service is held on Saturday. The Ark is opened and a Torah scroll is taken out and read.

Rabbi

The teacher or spiritual leader of the Synagogue. Sometimes he conducts the services (although lay people do so as well), and he acts as the judge in the Jewish courts and as the teacher. He would have studied for many years, and would be a man of great learning.

Mitzvot

This is the name given to the good works. It means praying, studying the Torah, giving to charities, keeping the ten commandments etc.

Tefillin

A small leather box containing writings from the Torah. The Orthodox Jew fastens one on to his head, to show that he thinks about God, and another onto his left arm to show that he loves God.

Tallit

This is the prayer shawl, worn by men, when they pray.

Yamulkah

This is the small skullcap. Some Jews wear it all the time, others wear it with the prayer shawl, when praying.

Kosher Food

Jews have very strict rules regarding food. Certain foods must not be eaten, such as pork, rabbit or shell-fish. (Read Leviticus, chapter 11.) Meat must be koshered. (i.e. the animal is killed with a knife, and the blood is drained away.) Meat and dairy products should not be eaten at the same meal. There should always be separate plates, pans and cutlery for milk and meat dishes in a Kosher kitchen.

Havdallah

Marks the end of Shabbat. The traditional plaited Havdallah candle is lit, and a box of sweet smelling spices is passed around for everyone to smell, to remind each other to take the sweet smell of Shabbat, into the week with them.

JEWISH FESTIVALS

Rosh Hashana

The Jewish New Year. It begins in the Hebrew month of Tishri. (That is, September or October). (See pages 17–21.)

Yom Kippur

The day of Atonement. A special day of fast when Jews ask God for the forgiveness of their sins. (See page 17.)

Sukkot

The week-long harvest festival that takes place in October. (See pages 66–68.)

Simhat Torah

Celebrating the Torah. Over the year, the Torah is read in the synagogue, from beginning to end. On this day, the end of the reading and the beginning of the re-reading is celebrated.

Hannukah

The Festival of Lights, held in December, celebrating the winning back of the Temple of Jerusalem. (See pages 69–71.)

Purim

The Festival of Purim or the Feast of Lots is celebrated in the Jewish month of Adar around February/March time. The teacher will find the account in the Bible (The Book of Esther). It is called the Feast of Lots, because Haman cast lots to 'choose the best day on which to kill the Jews'. (See pages 72–77)

Pesah

Passover. A special meal and the service known as Seder, marks the beginning of this seven or eight day celebration in the Spring. Find out about the special and symbolic representation of the food that is eaten at the Seder meal. (See picture below; and see also pages 78–82)

The Seder Table

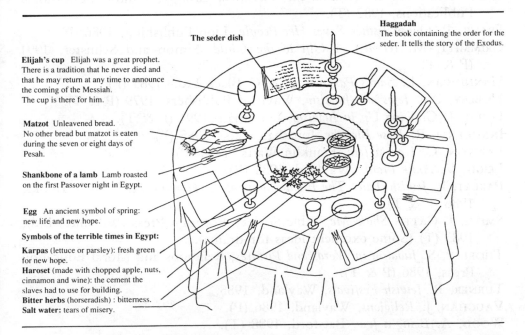

Haggadah
The book containing the order for the seder. It tells the story of the Exodus.

The seder dish

Elijah's cup Elijah was a great prophet. There is a tradition that he never died and that he may return at any time to announce the coming of the Messiah. The cup is there for him.

Matzot Unleavened bread. No other bread but matzot is eaten during the seven or eight days of Pesah.

Shankbone of a lamb Lamb roasted on the first Passover night in Egypt.

Egg An ancient symbol of spring: new life and new hope.

Symbols of the terrible times in Egypt:

Karpas (lettuce or parsley): fresh green for new hope.
Haroset (made with chopped apple, nuts, cinnamon and wine): the cement the slaves had to use for building.
Bitter herbs (horseradish) : bitterness.
Salt water: tears of misery.

Source: *Judaism in Words and Pictures*, by S. Thorley, RMEP, 1986 page 23. Reproduced by kind permission of Chansitor Publications Ltd.

Shavuot

This is held seven weeks later. It is a celebration of the giving of the Law at Mount Sinai. Why not make your own scrolls using two dowling rods with a piece of paper attached.

Resources

Books

BAILEY, J.R. *Founders, Prophets and Sacred Books*, Schofield & Sims Ltd., 1985 (T).

BAILEY, J.R. *Religious Buildings and Festivals*, Schofield & Sims Ltd., 1984 (T).

BARNETT, V. *A Jewish Family in Britain*, Religious and Moral Education Press, 1983 (P & T).

BERGEY, A. *The Great Promise*, Concordia Publishing House, Arch Books, 1968 (P).

CHARING, D. *The Jewish World*, Macdonald 1983 (P & T).

CHARING, D. *Visiting a Synagogue*, Lutterworth Educational, 1984 (P & T).

COLE, W.O. *Six Religions in the Twentieth Century*, Hulton Educational Publications, 1982 (T).

FRANK, P. *Queen Esther Saves Her People*, Lion Publishing, 1986 (P).

GRIMMITT, M. (*et al.*) *A Gift to the Child*, Simon and Schuster, 1991 (P & T)

HANNINGAN, L. *Sam's Passover*, A & C Black Ltd., 1985 (P).

HOBLEY, L.F. *Jews and Judaism*, Wayland Publishers, 1979 (P & T).

HOLM, J. *Growing Up in Judaism*, Longman, 1991 (P & T).

INNOCENTI, R. *Rose Blanche*, Jonathan Cape, 1985 (P).

LAWTON, C. *I am a Jew*, Franklin Watts, 1984 (P).

LEIGH, V. *Anne Frank*, Wayland, 1985 (P).

PARLAT, L. *Jewish Tales The Eight Lights of the Hanukkiya*, Beehive Books, 1986 (P & T).

SMITH, J. GATTIS *Show Me*, Bible Society Borough Press (Wiltshire) Ltd., 1985 (T) (Some excellent ideas for drama).

THORLEY, S. *Judaism in Words and Pictures*, Religious and Moral Education Press, 1986 (P & T).

TURNER, R. *Jewish Festivals*, Wayland, 1985.

VAUGHAN, J. *Religions*, Wayland, 1986 (P).

WOOD, A. *Being a Jew*, Batsford, 1988 (T).

(P) = Pupils
(T) = Teachers

Useful Addresses

Books & Information
The Jewish Museum Bookshop
Woburn House
Upper Woburn Place
London WC1H OEP

Cassette & Songbook mentioned on pages 35, 67, 75, 82, 136
Andrea Baron
6 Blenheim Gardens
Wallington
Surrey
Tel: 081–647–2274

Send for price list for the cassette and for the booklet, include the cost of postage and packing.

All other songbooks, CD's, cassettes
Jewish Music Distribution
PO Box 2268
Hendon
London NW4 3UW
Tel: 081 203 8046

Pronunciation Guide to Jewish Words

a	'a' as in 'fah'
ai	'ai' as in 'sigh'
ad/on/ai	'ad' as in 'bud'; 'on' as in 'on'; 'ai' as in 'sigh'
ad/on o/lam	'ad' as in 'bud'; 'on' as in 'on'; o as in 'no'; 'lam' as in 'dramb'
akh/shav	'akh' rhymes with 'Bach'; 'sh' as in 'shut'; 'av' as in 'halve'
a/ley/nu	'a' as in 'fah'; 'ley' as in 'lay'; 'nu' rhymes with 'shoe'
all/e	'all' as in 'pal'; 'e' as in 'led'
am/o	'am' as in 'lamb'; 'o' as in 'toe'
ar/on hak/o/desh	'ar' as in 'are'; 'on' as in 'on'; 'hak' as in 'back'; 'o' as in 'toe'; 'desh' rhymes with 'flesh'
ash/er	'ash' as in 'dash'; 'er' as in 'air'
az	pronounced 'as'
az/ai	'az' as in 'as'; 'ai' as in 'sigh'

Hebrew alphabet

L	KH	Y	T	KH	Z

לכיטחז

V	H	D	G	B	Silent

והדגבא

T	S/SH	R	K	TZ

תשרקצ

P/F	Silent	S	N	M

פעסנמ

KH	TZ	P/F	N	M

דץףן ס

Shalom שלום

Source: *My Belief: I am a Jew*, by C. Lawton published by Franklin Watts. 1984 Artwork by Tony Payne.

ba	'ba' as in 'bah'
bash/an/ah	'bash' rhymes with 'dash'; 'an' as in 'van'; 'ah' as in 'fah'
bim/ro/mav	'bim' rhymes with 'Tim'; 'ro' rhymes with 'toe'; 'mav rhymes with 'halve'
bit/fill/a	'bit' rhymes with 'fit'; 'fill' as in 'feel'; 'a' as in 'fah'
be-rosh hashan/a	'be' as in the phonetic sound 'b'; 'rosh' rhymes with 'gosh'; 'ha' as in 'h'; 'sh' as in 'shut'; 'anah' as in Anna
b'terem	'b' as in 'bat'; 'tere' rhymes with 'care'; 'em' as in the phonetic sound 'm'
ch	as in Bach
der	pronounced as phonetic sound 'd'
die	pronounced 'dee'
dov/en	'dov' pronounced phonetically; then add 'n'
dovt	'dov' pronounced phonetically; then add 't'
e	as in led
ë	as in they
Esther	pronounced Ester; silent 'h'
et	as in get
etz/li	'etz' rhymes with 'gets'; 'li' rhymes with 'tree'
gin/na	'g' as in 'give'; 'i' as 'see'; 'na' rhymes with 'fah'
go/ali	'go' as in 'go'; 'ali' rhymes with 'valley'
g'viati	'g' as in 'get'; 'v' as letter name 'V'; 'ati' rhymes with 'batty'
ha	as in 'fah'
ha/kol	'ha' as in 'fah'; 'kol' as in 'collar'
hall/el	'hall' rhymes with 'pal'; 'el' as in 'ale'
ha/lo	'ha' as in 'fah'; 'lo' as in 'low'
Haman	'Ha' as in 'hay'; 'man' rhymes with 'van'
Hann/u/kah	'Han' rhymes with 'ban'; 'u' as in 'you'; 'kah' as in 'kah'
h/as/do	guttural 'h'; 'as' as in 'has'; 'do' rhymes with 'toe'
h/as/i/dim	guttural 'h'; 'as' as in 'has'; 'i' as in 'me'; 'dim' as in 'dim'
hash/vi/i	'hash' rhymes with 'dash'; 'vi' rhymes with 'tea'; 'i' rhymes with tea
Hat/hach	'Hat' rhymes with 'hut'; 'hach' rhymes with 'Bach'
hatz/av	'hatz' as in 'hats'; 'av' as in 'halve'
hav/a na/gi/la	'have' as in 'halve'; 'a' rhymes with 'fah'; 'na' as in 'far'; 'gi' rhymes with 'tea'; 'la' as in 'fah'

ho/du l'ad/on/ai	'ho' rhymes with 'hoe'; 'du' as in 'you'; 'l'ad' as
ki tov	in 'lad'; 'on' as in 'on'; 'ai' as in 'sigh'; 'ki' rhymes with 'tea'; 'tov' as it sounds phonetically
hof	silent 'h'
i	as in 'me'
ken/er	'ken' rhymes with 'ten'; 'er' as in 'a'
k'/h/evtz/o	'k' as in 'Kate'; guttural 'h'; 'evtz' rhymes with 'bets'; 'o' as in 'toe'
k/ihl/ot	'k' as in 'Kate'; 'ihl' rhymes with 'heel'; 'ot' as in 'lot'
klep/pen	'klep' as it sounds phonetically; 'pen' rhymes with 'den'
klept	as it sounds phonetically; then add a 't'
kol	like collar
ko/sher	'ko' rhymes with 'toe'; 'sher' rhymes with 'fur'
l'eyt	pronounced 'late'
l'hit/a/re/ah	'l' as in 'lah'; 'hit' as in 'heat'; 'a' as in 'fah'; 're' as in 'ray'; 'ah' as in 'fah'
libb/e/nu	'libb' as in Lee(b); 'e' as in 'say'; 'nu' as in 'you'
mal/ah	'mal' rhymes with 'mall'; 'ah' as in 'fah'
mat/hil/a	'mat' rhymes with 'cat'; 'hil' as in 'heel'; 'a' as in 'fah'
mel/e/h	'mel' rhymes with 'bell'; 'e' as in 'get'; guttural 'h'
men/or/ah	'men' rhymes with 'mun'; 'or' as in 'or'; 'ah' as in 'fah'
m'/hu/bad	'm' sounded phonetically; guttural 'h'; 'u' rhymes with 'do'; 'bad' as in 'sad'
mi/kkol	'mi' rhymes with 'tea'; 'kkol' as in 'collar'
m'/lah/te/ha	'm' sounded phonetically; 'lah' pronounced 'l'; guttural 'h'; 'te' rhymes with 'say'; 'ha' as in 'fah'
Mor/dec/ai	'Mor' rhymes with 'saw'; 'd' as in the phonetic sound 'd'; guttural 'c'; 'ai' rhymes with 'sigh'
na'a/sah	'na'a' rhymes 'bah'; 'sah' rhymes with 'fah'
nik/ra	'nik' rhymes with 'tick'; 'ra' rhymes with 'fah'
niv/ra	'niv' rhymes with 'give'; 'ra' rhymes with 'fah'
no/ra	'no' as in 'gnaw'; 'ra'; as in 'rah'
nosh/an/a	'nosh' rhymes with 'gosh'; 'an' rhymes with 'fan'; 'a' as in 'fah'
o	as in 'boat'
o/gena	'o' as in 'toe'; 'g' as in 'give'; 'en' rhymes with 'fen'; 'a' as in 'fah'

o/la/mim	'o' as in 'toe'; 'la' as in 'fah'; 'mim' rhymes with 'meem'
o/seh	'o' as in 'toe'; 'sey' as in 'say'
oz v'shalom	'oz' as in Wizard of Oz'; 'v' as in the letter name 'V'; 'shal' as in 'shall'; 'lom' rhymes with 'mom'
pa/am	'pa' as in 'pah'; 'am' rhymes with 'Sam'
par/ha	'par' rhymes with 'far'; guttural 'h'; 'ha' rhymes with 'cah'
pe/sah	'pe' as in 'pay'; 'sah' as in 'a', guttural 'h'
pi/tom	'pi' rhymes with 'tea'; 'tom' as in 'Tom'
pu/rim	'pu' as in 'pooh'; 'rim' as in 'rim'
Reb/be	'Reb' rhymes with 'deb'; 'be' as in the letter name 'b'
Rab/bi	'Rab' rhymes with 'dab'; 'bi' rhymes with 'sigh'
rak	'ra' rhymes with 'fah'; silent 'k'
rosh hash/an/a	'rosh' rhymes with 'gosh'; 'hash' rhymes with 'dash'; 'an' as in 'fan'; 'a' as in 'fah'
sam/e/ah	'sam' rhymes with 'dram'; 'e' rhymes with 'say'; 'ah' as in 'fah', guttural 'h'
setav	pronounced saav; long 'aa' sound
shabat	'sh' as in 'shut'; 'a' as in 'halve'; 'ba' as in 'fah'; 't' is pronounced
shal/om	'shal' rhymes with 'shall'; 'om' rhymes with 'mom'
shav/u/ot	'sh' as in 'shut'; 'av' as in 'have'; 'u' as in 'oo'; 't' as in 'top'
she/shet	'she' as in 'sheh'; 'shet' rhymes with 'get'
shluf/en	'shluf' pronounced phonetically and then add 'n'
shluf/t	'shluf' pronounced phonetically and add the 't'
sh'/mo	'sh' as in 'shut'; 'mo' rhymes with 'toe'
sho/far	'sho' rhymes with 'toe'; 'far' as in 'far'
sho/shan/a	'sho' rhymes with 'show'; 'shan' as it sounds phonetically; 'a' as in 'fah'
sh/ve/gen	'sh' as in 'shut'; 've' rhymes with 'day'; 'g' as in 'get'; 'en' like the letter name 'N'
shveygt	'shvetygt' rhymes with 'fate'
su/kkot	'su' as in 'Sue'; 'kkot' as in 'cot'
ta/a/seh	'ta' as in 'ta'; 'a' as in 'ah'; 'sey' as in 'say'
ta/llit	'ta' as in 'fah'; 'llit' as in 'feet'
tash/lich	'tash' rhymes with 'dash'; 'lich' as in 'leek'; guttural final 'h'
te/fill/in	'te' pronounced as phonetic 't'; 'fill' as in 'fill'; 'in' rhymes with 'bin'

te/he	'te' as in 'say'; 'he' as in 'hay'
to/rah	'to' rhymes with 'door'; 'rah' rhymes with 'fah'
tzur	pronounced 'tz' plus 'oor'
um'/va/de/ah	'um' as in 'locum'; 'va' as in 'fah'; 'de' as in 'day'; 'ah' as in 'fah'
u'/ru/a/him	'u' as in 'oo'; 'ru' as in 'rue'; 'a' as in 'fah'; guttural 'h'; 'him' rhymes with 'Tim'
v'/ah/a/rei	'v' as in 'van'; 'ah' as in 'a'; guttural 'h'; 'a' as in 'up'; 'rei' rhymes with 'day'
va/sh/ti	'va' as in 'vah'; 'sh' as in 'shut', 'ti' rhymes with 'tea'
ve/shon/a	've' as in the phonetic sound 'v'; 'shon' as in 'shown'; 'a' as in 'ah'
vey/nen	'vey' rhymes with 'day'; 'nen' as in the phonetic sound 'n'
veynt	rhymes with faint
v'/im/ru	'v' as in 'van'; 'im' as in 'Tim'; 'ru' rhymes with 'shoe'
v'/nis/'m/hah	'v' rhymes with 'day'; 'nis' rhymes with 'niece'; 'm' as sounded phonetically; 'hah' as in 'fah'
vo	rhymes with 'toe'
v'yom	'v' as in 'van'; 'yom' rhymes with 'mom'
ya'/a/seh	'ya' as in 'yah', 'a' as in 'ah'; 'sey' rhymes with 'say'
yad	as in yah'd
ya/fa	'ya' as in 'yah'; 'fa' as in 'fah'
ya/min	'ya' as in 'yah'; 'min' rhymes with 'been'
ya/mul/kah	'ya' as in 'yah'; 'mul' as in 'mool'; kah' as in 'fah'
Yis/r/ael	Yis' as it sounds; 'r' as in 'ray'; 'ael' as in 'ale'
yi/teyn	'y' as in 'yellow'; 'i' rhymes with 'see'; 'teyn' rhymes with 'ten'
yom kip/pur	'y' as in 'yellow'; 'yom' rhymes with 'mom'; 'kip' rhymes with 'keep'; 'pur' rhymes with 'poor'
yom/ru	'yom' rhymes with 'mom'; 'ru' as in 'you'
yom zeh m'/hu/bad	'yom' rhymes with 'mom'; 'zeh' rhymes with 'day' 'm' as phonetic sound; guttural 'h'; 'hu' rhymes with 'do'; 'bad' as in 'bah'd'
y't zir	'y't' as in 'fit'; 'zir' rhymes with 'dear'
y'/va/reh	'y' as in phonetic sound 'y'; 'va' as in 'fah'; 're' as in 'red'; guttural 'h'
ze	rhymes with 'zeh'
zingen	like 'singin' but with a 'z'

Buddhism

Background Information

The Buddha or 'Enlightened One'

The Buddha was born in the fifth or sixth century BCE. According to tradition, he was known as Siddhārtha Gautama, the son of a north Indian King. He married Yashodharā and lived a life of luxury, protected from the outside world. One day, he went outside the palace and saw four people who changed his life. He saw a sick man, an old man, a dead man and a Holy man. He left home in search of the meaning of suffering. For six years, he stayed with five Holy Men, fasting, and enduring great hardship, almost to the point of death. Then one day, in deep meditation, sitting under a tree, his enlightenment came. From this time onwards, he was known as the Buddha, or 'Enlightened One' and he began his teaching. See the Four Noble Truths and the Eight Fold Path below.

The Four Noble Truths

The Buddha taught that:—

1 All life involves suffering.
2 Suffering is due to selfishness.
3 If selfishness is subjugated, suffering will stop.
4 The way to end suffering is to follow the Eight Fold Path.

The Eight Fold Path

1 Right Understanding
2 Right Thought   } wisdom
3 Right speech
4 Right action   } morality
5 Right livelihood
6 Right mental effort
7 Right mindfulness   } meditation
8 Right concentration

(From: *Founders, Prophets and Sacred Books* by J.R. Bailey)

Several Types of Buddhism Today

According to tradition, the Buddha lived for eighty years. Attempts to clarify and systematise his teaching in the centuries after his death, led eventually, to two broad interpretations of what Buddhism is finally all about. The first approach, is represented in modern Buddhism by the Theravāda tradition, the Doctrine of the Elders, found particularly in Sri Lanka and South East Asia. This form of Buddhism, claims to represent faithfully, the pure original teachings of the Buddha, and places particular emphasis on a monastic tradition which leads eventually to individual and personal enlightenment for those who follow the Buddha's path. The other approach, called itself 'Mahāyāna Buddhism', the 'Great Vehicle', and is found nowadays particularly in China, Japan, and the other countries of East Asia, and Tibet. Here, although the form of Buddhism represented by Theravāda is not denied, the emphasis is on attaining the very same enlightenment as the Buddha, in order to be able to better benefit all sentient beings. Thus in Mahāyāna Buddhism, kindness to others becomes a particularly prominent theme. (Williams)

Sūtra

Sūtra is the sanskrit of the Pali 'Sutta'. It is the name given to the collection of the Buddha's discourses.

Vinaya

These are the rules for monastic life.

Jātaka (birth) Tales

Jātaka tales are stories relating to the Buddha's previous lives on the path to enlightenment.

BUDDHIST FAMILY LIFE

Background Information

Birth Rites

Often there is no special ceremony to become a Buddhist, (although, for those who are older, there is a ceremony of 'Taking Refuge' in Tibetan Buddhism). Sometimes, a family will invite a Buddhist monk to the house to bless the child, but basically a person becomes a Buddhist by following the Eight Fold Path.

A Duty

Buddhist parents feel that they have a duty to give their children a good education, teaching them to be kind to all living creatures; to arrange their marriage; to give money and food to Buddhist monks.

The Buddha Statues

Buddhists will often have a statue of the Buddha in their own home. They show respect by bowing before their statue and will often place flowers in front of their statue. Candles and incense are burnt as a symbol of the light that the Buddha shed with his teaching. (see page 190.)

Temple or Vihāra

Buddhists do not have a set time or day to go to the temple, although they will often visit the temple on full moon days and special festival days.

Monks (Bhikkhus) & Nuns (Bhikkhunis) in the Theravāda Tradition

Monks and Nuns learn to have few possessions, such as a simple robe and an alms bowl. They have no money of their own and are given all their food. They also shave their heads. Monks must beg for all their food. The rules which the monks live by are called the Basic Precepts.

1 Not to destroy or harm life
2 Not to steal

3 The rule of chastity which is not to have sexual relations or marry.
4 Not to tell lies
5 Not to take intoxicating drinks
6 Not to eat other than at meal times
7 Not to go to entertainments like shows, with dancing or music
8 Not to wear perfumes or scents or wear ornaments and decoration
9 Not to sleep on comfortable raised beds
10 Not to accept or handle gold or silver

(From: *Buddhists and Buddhism* by M. Patrick published by Wayland, 1982, page 33.)

In general, all Buddhist people aspire to observe the first five of these rules. Rule 3 is adapted to mean irresponsible sexual relations. A further three rules are observed by families on special Buddhist Holy days.

Meditation

Many Buddhists meditate or think deeply in their own homes. The aim of meditation is to clear the mind of feelings of greed, hatred or laziness and to fill the mind with love and kind thoughts towards others. Also to understand better, the way things are.

Nirvāna

Is the highest state of happiness which all Buddhist aim to achieve.

Food

Some Buddhists are vegetarians and will not eat any meat or fish or eggs. Others do eat meat.

Clothes

Buddhists usually wear the national dress from their country of origin. For instance, if a Buddhist comes from India, a sari is worn by the women. Men in England, will usually wear western clothes. On full moon days, simple white clothes are sometimes worn. (A Theravāda tradition).

BUDDHIST FESTIVALS

Fin.! out all about Buddhist Festivals. In general, they are held at the time of full moon, and vary from Country to Country. Some of the following are observed in Sri Lanka.

Vesākha

This is the most important full moon festival held in April or May. It is a celebration of the Buddha's birth, his Enlightenment and his death. It is also the Buddhist New Year. (See pages 22–23).

Jetthamāsa

The month of June, celebrates the spread of Buddhism from India to other countries.

Asālha

In the month of July, there is a celebration in memory of the Buddha leaving home and preaching his first sermon.

Kathina

The month of November, is remembered as the month when the Buddha sent his first 60 disciples to spread his message around India. It also commemorates, the making of a new robe on a frame called a Kathina, with the Buddha. (See pages 83–84).

Phussa

This takes place in January. It is a first celebration of the Buddha's first visit to Sri Lanka.

Resources

Books

BAILEY, J.R. *Founders, Prophets and Sacred Books*, Schofield and Sims Ltd., 1985 (T).

BANCROFT, A. *The Buddhist World*, Macdonald, 1984 (P & T).

COLE, W.O. (Ed.) *Religion in the Multi-faith School*, Hulton Educational Publications Ltd., 1983 (T).

LING, T. *Buddhism*, Ward Lock Educational, 1970 (T).

MORGAN, P. *Being a Buddhist*, Batsford, 1989 (T).

MORGAN, P. *Buddhism in the Twentieth Century*, Hulton.

MORGAN, P. *Buddhist Stories*, (P & T).   ⎫ available from: Westminster
            Buddhist Iconography, (T).   ⎬ College North Hinksey,
                                            ⎭ Oxford OX2 9AT

PATRICK, M. *Buddhists and Buddhism*, Wayland, 1982 (P & T).

SAMARASEKARA, D. *I am a Buddhist*, Franklin Watts, 1986 (P).

SNELLING, J. *Buddhism*, Wayland, 1986 (P & T).

SNELLING, J. *Buddhist Festivals*, Wayland, 1985 (P & T).

TRIGGS, T.D. *Founders of Religions*, Wayland, 1981 (T & P).

VAUGHAN, J. *Religions*, Wayland, 1986 (P).

WILLIAMS, P. *Mahāyāna Buddhism. The Doctrinal Foundations*, Routledge, 1989 (For advanced study).

(P) = Pupils
(T) = Teachers

Useful Address

The Buddhist Society
58, Eccleston Square
London SW1V 1PH

Pronunciation Guide to Buddhist Words

A/sāl/ha	'A' as in 'fah'; 'sāl' rhymes with 'Carl'; 'ha' as in 'hah'
Bhik/khun/is	'Bhik' as in 'bick'; 'khun' rhymes with 'soon'; 'is' as in 'ease'
Bhik/khus	'Bhik' as in 'bick'; 'khus' as in 'queues'
Bud/dha	'Bud' as in 'pud'; 'dha' as in 'duh'
Dev/ad/atta	'Dev' as it is pronounced phonetically; 'ad' as in 'hard' 'atta' as in 'utter'
Jāt/a/ka	'Jāt' rhymes with 'part'; 'a' as in 'A'; 'ka' as in 'kuh'
Jett/ha/mā/sa	'Jett' as in 'jet'; 'ha' as in 'hut'; 'ma' as in 'far'; 'sa' as in 'suh'

Kat/hin/a	'Kat' as in 'cat'; 'hin' rhymes with 'been'; 'a' as in 'uh'
Ma/hā/yāna	'Ma' plus 'hā' as in 'car'; 'yāna' rhymes with 'farmer'
Man/tras	'Man' as in 'man'; 'tras' rhymes with 'daz'
Nir/vāna	'Nir' as in 'near'; 'vāna' rhymes with farmer'
Pā/li	'Pā' as in 'car'; 'li' rhymes with 'tree'
Phu/ssa	'Phu' rhymes with 'do' (silent 'h'); 'ssa' as in 'suh'
Sam/sā/ra	'Sam' as in 'sang'; 'sā' rhymes with 'car'; 'ra' as in 'ruh'
San/skrit	'San' rhymes with 'fan'; 'skrit' rhymes with 'writ'
Sidd/hārth/a	'Sidd' as in the name; 'hārth' as in 'heart'; 'a' as in 'uh';
Gaut/a/ma	'Gaut' as in 'gout'; 'a' as in 'far'; 'ma' as in 'muh'
Sūt/ra	'Sūt' as in 'suit'; 'ra' as in 'rah'
Sut/ta	'Sut' as in 'put'; 'ta' as in 'tah'
Thera/vāda	'Thera' as in 'terror' (silent 'h'); 'vāda' rhymes with 'larder'
Ve/sāk/ha	'Ve' rhymes with 'bay'; 'sāk' as in 'ark'; 'ha' as in 'huh'
Vi/hā/ra	'Vi'as in 'vih'; 'hā' as in 'hah'; 'ra' as in 'rut'
Vin/ay/a	'Vin' rhymes with 'bin'; 'ay' as in 'eye'; 'a' as in 'hah'
Yash/o/dha/rā	'Yash' rhymes with 'mass'; 'o' as in 'toe'; 'dha' as in 'far'; 'rā' as in 'car'

Buddha statues showing different hand positions

Turning the wheel of the law.

Right hand raised in protective gesture.

Teaching pose.

Hand touching the earth, calling the earth
to witness his enlightenment.

Meditation pose.

Hinduism

Background Information

There is no one founder, central figure or sacred book. Hinduism developed over many centuries and takes its name from the River Indus in North West India. (For more detailed information, see the book list at the end of this section.) A brief description of the place of the gods and goddesses is given below.

One god or thirty-three million gods

Both statements would be true. Many Hindus believe in Brahman or World Soul, but they also believe in many gods and goddesses, who are aspects of World Soul. Worshippers seem to fall into three main groups; those who see Lord Vishnu (or one of his incarnations) as their main god; those who see Shiva as their main god; and those who see the mother goddess as more powerful, than all the other gods.

Lord Vishnu

Lord Vishnu is believed to have existed before the world was created. He is often worshipped in the form of one of his many avatars or incarnations, such as the gods, Ram or Krishna. Lord Vishnu is depicted with four hands, in which he holds a conch shell, a lotus, a mace and a discus. He takes on one of his many different forms when evil threatens the world.

Lord Shiva

Shiva is sometimes called Lord of the Dance; his energy keeps the world turning throughout eternity, but eventually his energy will bring about the destruction of the world, before it is re-created again and again through his dance. He is often depicted as a holy man, wearing prayer beads and carrying a snake, a three-pronged spear and an axe. In the middle of his forehead he has a third eye.

The mother goddess or devi

For some Hindus, the goddess is the central deity (Bahree, page 14 *The Hindu World*, Macdonald). She is thought to protect mothers and children, and once again, she is worshipped in many forms. She is often depicted as the beautiful, kind, mother goddess. She is *Parvati* the wife of Shiva. Sometimes, she takes the form of the all-powerful warrior goddess *Durga*, with her ten arms, who rides on the back of a lion, to slay the evil demon king. (see page 95) At yet other times, she is depicted as the goddess *Kali* who brings storms and floods, earthquakes and illnesses. As *Lakshmi*, she is the wife of Vishnu and the goddess of good fortune, wealth and beauty. She is worshipped at the festival of Diwali. She is often depicted standing or sitting on a lotus blossom, holding the conch shell and lotus, similar to the ones that her husband holds.

Other Deities

Brahma

He is regarded as equal with Lord Vishnu and Lord Shiva. He is usually depicted with four faces riding on a swan. In his hands, he carries a book, a sceptre and an alms bowl.

Saraswati

She is the beautiful wife of Brahma and she is also depicted riding on a swan, carrying a musical instrument and a book, as she is the goddess of music, literature and art.

Hanuman

He is the monkey god, who helped Ram rescue his wife Sita, from the demon king. (See pages 85–88 for this story.)

Ganesh

He is the elephant-headed god, son of the goddess Parvati. He is often depicted riding on a rat. He is the remover of obstacles; often worshippers will pray to Lord Ganesh, before starting a new job. (see page 201)

Surya

He is the sun god, who is often depicted driving his sun chariot across the sky during the day.

Chandra

He is the moon god, who travels the sky by night.

Agni

He is the god of fire, and he is present wherever there is a fire.

Prasad

Is the food offered to the gods and then eaten by the worshippers.

Hindu Literature

Vedas is the name given to some of the most ancient Hindu literature. It consists of four collections of hymns known as Rig, Sama, Yajur and Atharvan. Other Hindu literature includes the Brahmanas (priestly writings), Aranyakas (forest stories) and Upanishads (the discussions with Gurus and Holy men). The Bhagavad Gita, part of the famous epic called Mahabharata, is Krishna's sermon on duty.

Sanskrit

This is the ancient written language which is still used today for ritual purposes.

Mandir

This is the name given to the Hindu temple, and domestic shrines. Many Hindus worship images or pictures of Gods in their own homes. Everybody must take off their shoes outside the temple as a mark of respect.

HINDU FAMILY LIFE

Naming Ceremony

In Hindu culture, there are many different naming ceremonies, according to the caste or region where the child is born. However, most name-giving ceremonies are determined by the child's own horoscope. The ceremony takes place after the child's birth and before his first birthday, when the family priest works out the baby's exact horoscope. Using this information, he will select the initial letter for the child's name. Hindu names, usually have a special meaning i.e. if the letter is 'R', for instance, then the child may be named Ram, after one of the gods (see Assembly on page 102).

Mundan

This is the ceremony when a boy's head is shaved. Before this, his hair has not been cut at all. In the mundan, families feel that the last traces of his previous life are removed. There are many different customs regarding the mundan. In the Punjab region, for instance, Hindus believe the ceremony should take place during the first year of life before the child's first birthday or certainly before his third or fifth birthday, providing that no relative has died during the previous year. (Celebrations are delayed to the third or fifth year of life, if there has been a death in the family, because no celebration can take place for a full year after a death). A barber attends and shaves the child's head. Then the child is washed and dressed in new clothes, usually bought by the child's maternal uncle. The child receives gifts of money from all who attend the ceremony.

Hindu Family and Caste System

Families vary greatly according to caste, sect, linguistic group, and whether they are westernized, urban or rural. Brahmins are the highest caste; the priestly caste. Kshatriyas are the military caste. Vaishyas are the caste that works mainly in trade or farming. Shudras are the servants of the other castes. The lowest caste is known as the Untouchables.

Very occasionally, there are inter-caste marriages and some members of lower castes have highly paid jobs. But some of the older generation find it difficult to break with tradition and some Hindus would feel it was unthinkable even to eat with a member of a different caste.

Sari

This is the name given to the beautiful dress worn by many Hindu women and girls. It is made from one piece of material which is approximately 130 centimetres wide and 6 metres long. The cloth is wound around the waist, pleated and then tucked into an underskirt, allowing the remaining part of the material to be draped across the shoulder in different styles. In Britain today, both men and women, boys and girls often wear western clothes, although some women wear their sari daily and others wear it only for special occasions.

Food

Some Hindus are vegetarians as they believe it is wrong to kill any living creature. However, many Hindus do eat meat although they may not eat beef as the cow is a sacred animal. The reason for this, is the cow is often described as a mother, because she gives us milk to drink. Vegetables are cooked with all kinds of spices. As food was traditionally eaten with the hands, that is, without knives and forks, there are very strict rules about washing hands before and after each meal.

HINDU FESTIVALS

Find out about Hindu Festivals. Include some of the ones listed below. There are some very useful books to help you in the resources section.

Navratri

This means nine nights. The festival takes place following the new moon in September/October. At this time, Hindus worship the goddess. In one of her many forms she is called Durga (with her ten arms).

In a sense, this festival is similar to Harvest Festival in Britain as the farming community in India await harvest after the hard work on the land during the summer and the monsoon rains (see pages 94–95).

Dussehra

This is the tenth day of the above festival. In some parts of India young children are taught the alphabet on this day. In other parts the story of Ram and Sita is acted out. Huge models of Ravan, the demon King, are made and then ceremoniously burnt. Why not try to write some Hindi script or make a huge effigy of Ravan (see page 201 for an example of Hindi script).

Diwali

The festival of lights (late October). In some parts of India, this festival is regarded as a celebration of the renewal of life; in other parts it is regarded as the festival for protection against King Bali, the King of the underworld. King Bali could only rule where there was no light, so everyone makes sure that many lamps keep him away. In yet other parts of India, the festival, is a celebration of the return of Ram, when everyone lit lamps to guide him home after his exile, and Ram and Sita were crowned King and Queen. (see pages 85–88).

Lakshmi, the Goddess of Wealth, is also worshipped at this time, and many Hindus light candles, to welcome her into their homes.

Why not make a special candle for this occasion, known as diva/diwa. (Traditionally, a small clay saucer, with a cotton wool wick, soaked in clarified butter, would be used. Diwali takes its name from these little candles or diva). Or re-enact the play of Ram and Sita in your school assembly (see pages 85–88). Perhaps you could make masks for Ram, Sita, Ravan (with ten heads) and Hanuman, the monkey god who helped Ram.

Some families send Diwali cards to each other, or paint rangoli patterns of welcome on their doorsteps. Others paint Mehndi patterns on their hands. Find out about these traditions and make your own cards and patterns.

Holi

Celebrates the coming of Spring. Revellers squirt coloured water at each other. Agni the God of Fire is worshipped by lighting huge bonfires and dancing around the fires. The story of Prince Prahlad and Princess Holika is retold. Find out about this exciting story by reading *Celebrations* by C. Collinson and C. Miller. (see page 99) or read, *Holi, Festival of Spring*, by O. Bennett.

Janmashtami

The birthday of Lord Krishna, is celebrated in August, by waiting up until midnight, the time that it is thought that Lord Krishna was born. Special sweets are given to one another and stories about Lord Krishna are told.

Resources

AGGARWAL, M. *I am a Hindu*, Franklin Watts, 1984 (P).

BAHREE, P. *The Hindu World*, Macdonald, 1982 (P & T).

BAILEY, J.R. *Founders, Prophets and Sacred Books*, Schofield & Sims Ltd., 1985 (T).

BAILEY, J.R. *Religions Buildings and Festivals*, Schofield & Sims Ltd., 1984 (T).

BENNETT, O *Festival! Diwali*, Macmillan Education Ltd., 1986 (P & T).

BOND, R. *The Adventures of Rama and Sita*, Julia MacRae Books, 1987 (P).

COLE, W.O. (Ed.) *Religion in the Multi-Faith School*, Hulton Educational Publications Ltd., 1983 (T).

COLE, W.O. *Six Religions in the Twentieth Century*, Hulton Educational Publications Ltd., 1982 (T).

COLLINSON, C. and MILLER, C. *Celebrations*, Edward Arnold, 1985 (P & T).

CROMPTON, Y. *Hinduism*, Ward Lock Educational, 1971 (T).

DESHPANDE, C. *Diwali*, A. & C. Black, 1985 (P).

GRIMMITT, M. (*et al.*), *A Gift to the Child*, Simon and Schuster, 1991 (P & T).

HEASLIP, P.C. *Chapatis Not Chips*, Methuen Children's Book, 1987 (P).

Hirst, J. *Growing Up in Hinduism*, Longman, 1991 (P & T).

HUNTER, N. *Great Lives, Gandhi*, Wayland 1986 (T).

JACKSON, R. and KILLINGLEY, D. *Approaches to Hinduism*, John Murray, 1988 (T).

JACKSON, R. and NESBITT, E. *Listening to Hindus*, Unwin Hyman, 1990 (P & T).

JAFFREY, M. *Seasons of Splendour*, Pavilion Books Ltd, 1985 (P & T).

KANITKAR, V.P. *Hindu Stories*, Wayland, 1986 (P & T).

KANITKAR, V.P. *Hindu Festivals and Sacrements*, Pbk, 1984 (T).

KILLINGLEY, D. *A Handbook of Hinduism*, Grevatt & Grevatt 1984 (T).

MITTER, P. *Hindus and Hinduism*, Wayland, 1982 (P & T).

MITTER, P. *Hindu Festivals*, Wayland, 1985 (P).

RAY, S. *A Hindu Family in Britain*, Religious and Moral Education Press, 1985 (P & T).

SINGH, R. *The Indian Story Book*, Heinemann, 1984 (P).

SOLOMON, J. *Sweet-tooth Sunil*, Hamish Hamilton, 1984 (P).

THOMSON, R. *My Class at Diwali*, Franklin Watts, 1986 (P).

(P) = Pupils

(T) = Teachers

Useful Addresses:

Hindu Centre

39 Grafton Terrace

London NW5 4JA

Commonwealth Institute
Kensington High Street
London W8 6NQ

Oxfam Education Dept.,
274 Banbury Road
Oxford

Resources

Slides of a Hindu Wedding available from:

The Slide Centre,
Ilton,
Ilminster,
Somerset,
TAI9 9HS

C.E.M video: 'Hinduism through the eyes of Hindu children'

C.E.M.
Royal Buildings
Victoria Street,
Derby
DE1 1GW

Video available from:

Chansitor Publications
St. Mary's Works,
St. Mary's Plain
Norwich;
NR3 3BH

A good supplier of artefacts and pictures is:

Suresh Shah
Shah Pan House
523 Foleshill Road,
Coventry.

Pronunciation Guide to Hindu Words

An/na Prash/an	'An' rhymes with 'un' as in 'undo'; 'na' rhymes with 'far'; 'Prash' as in 'rush'; 'an' as in 'un'.
Bha/rat	'Bha' as in 'but'; 'rat' as in 'rut'.
Diw/a/li	'Diw' rhymes with 'give'; 'a' as in 'far', 'li' rhymes with 'see'.
Duss/eh/ra	'Duss' rhymes with 'thus'; 'e' as in 'let'; 'ra' as in 'far'.
Gan/esha	'Gan' is pronounced 'gun'; 'esh' rhymes with 'aish' as in 'facial'; silent 'a'.
Han/u/man	'Han' rhymes with 'Hun'; 'u' as in 'moo'; 'man' rhymes with 'calm'.
Ho/li	Pronounced 'holy'.
Ho/lik/a	'Ho' as in 'hoe'; 'lik' as in 'tick'; 'a' as in 'calm'.
Jan/mash/ta/mi	'Jan' as in 'gun'; 'mash' as in 'marsh'; 'ta' as in 'far'; 'mi' rhymes with 'see'.
Ka/li	'Ka' as in 'car'; 'li' rhymes with 'see'.
Krish/na	'Krish' rhymes with 'dish'; 'na' rhymes with 'far'.
Laksh/mi	'Laksh' is pronounced 'Lucksh'; 'mi' rhymes with 'see'.
Lank/a	'Lank' is pronounced 'Lunk'; 'a' as in 'calm'.
Laxsh/man	'Laxsh' is pronounced 'Lucksh'; 'man' rhymes with 'mun'.
Man/dir	'Man' rhymes with 'mun'; 'dir' rhymes with 'deer'.
Nav/ra/tri	'Nav' is pronounced 'Nuv'; 'ra' as in 'far'; 'tri' rhymes with 'see'.
Par/vat/i	'Par' rhymes with 'far'; 'vat' as in 'rut'; 'i' rhymes with 'see'.
Prah/lad	'Prah' as in 'but'; 'lad' as in 'calm'.
Pra/sad	'Pra' as in 'uh'; 'sad' as in 'guard'.
Rama	'Ram' rhymes with 'calm'. Silent 'a'.
Ra/vana	'Ra' as in 'far'; 'van' as in 'fun'. Silent 'a'.
Shiv/a	'Shiv' rhymes with 'live'; 'a' as in 'cat'.
Si/ta	'Si' rhymes with 'see'; 'ta' as in 'far'.
Vish/nu	'Vish' rhymes with 'fish', 'nu' rhymes with 'moo'.

The Hindi Script

A	Á	I	Ī	U
अ	आ	इ	ई	उ

Ū	ṚI	ṚĪ	LṚI	
ऊ	ऋ	ॠ	लृ	

É	AI	O	AU	(Ṃ)
ए	ऐ	ओ	औ	अं

Ḥ	K	KH	G	GH
अः	क	ख	ग	घ

Ṅ	C	CH	J	JH
ङ	च	छ	ज	झ

Ñ	Ṭ	ṬH	Ḍ	ḌH
ञ	ट	ठ	ड	ढ

Ṇ	T	TH	D	DH
ण	त	थ	द	ध

N	P	PH	B	BH
न	प	फ	ब	भ

M	Y	R	L	V(W)
म	य	र	ल	व

SH	Ṣ	S	H	KSH
श	ष	स	ह	क्ष

TR	JÑ(GÑ)			
त्र	ज्ञ			

Source: *My Belief: I am a Hindu* by M. Aggarwal Franklin Watts, 1984 artwork by Tony Payne.

Ganesh, the Remover of Obstacles

Source: Ann and Bury Peerless – Slide Resources and Picture Library

Islam

MUSLIM FAMILY LIFE

Background Information

Birth Rites

A Muslim child is a member of the Faith from birth. These words are spoken in the ears of the child at birth:
'La illah illa Allah Muhammad Abduhu wa rassoulu hu'. 'There is no God but Allah and Muhammad is his servant and Prophet'.
The child is circumcised soon after birth. About seven days later, in Muslim countries, there is a naming ceremony called 'Aqiqa'. The child's head is shaved, and a sacrifice of two sheep (or goats) is made for a boy child. A sacrifice of one sheep is made for a girl, and the meat is given to poor people. (Hoad, A. *Islam*, published by Wayland, 1986.)

Muhammad

Respect is paid to Muhammad, by saying the words 'Peace be upon him', whenever his name is mentioned.
He was born in Arabia, in the City of Makkah, (Mecca) in 570 A.D. The people worshipped many Gods, at that time, but when Muhammad was about forty years old, he was told by the Angel Jibra'il that he was to become Allah's messenger and that he should teach the people that there is only one God.

Al-Qur'an

This is the Holy book of the Muslim people. As Muhammad could not read or write, he had to learn by heart and recite all the messages from Allah. These were later written down and became known as the Qur'an (Koran).

The Hadith

The other important books for Muslims are called the Hadith. These are the books containing the accounts of Muhammad's doings and sayings.

Islam

This is an Arabic word. It is the name given to the Muslim religion and means submission to God.

The Five Pillars of Islam

Every Muslim must carry out these five duties.

1   *A Muslim must say, and act accordingly, that: 'There is only one God and Muhammad is his prophet'* (or messenger). (Thorley, S. *Islam in Words and Pictures*, RMEP, 1982)
2   *A Muslim must pray five times each day. Fajr* is the prayer said at dawn. *Zuhr* is the midday prayer. *Asr* is said in the afternoon. *Maghrib* is the prayer to be said at sunset. *I'sha* is said approximately an hour and a half later.
    Hands, mouth, nose, face, arms, head, ears, neck, and feet must be washed before each prayer.
    The Muezzin calls people to prayer from the top of the minaret of the mosque.
3   *Zakat* — every Muslim must give alms to the poor. Approximately $2\frac{1}{2}$ per cent of their savings is given every year.
4   *Fasting or Sawm* — During the month of Ramadan each year a Muslim must fast between dawn and sunset.
5   *Hajj* — It is the duty of every Muslim to make a pilgrimage to Makkah at least once during his lifetime, if he can afford it.

Mosque

This is the Muslim place of worship. Shoes must be removed as a mark of respect for God. (It also keeps the floors clean, as foreheads touch the ground in prayer). Prayer mats are used. These must face Makkah. The Mihrab is an alcove which shows the direction of Makkah. There are no chairs, statues or pictures of living creatures in the Mosque, so that the people cannot be distracted from worshipping God. Women pray in a different part of the Mosque. Sometimes prayer beads are used. There are usually 33 beads, to remind Muslims, of the 99 names of God, in the Qur'an. For example, God the Merciful etc.

Imam

This is the man who leads the prayers.

Al-Wudhu

This is the name given to the washing ritual before praying.

Food

Muslims have very strict rules regarding food. Pork is forbidden and alcohol is forbidden. Only meat from animals that have been killed by cutting the throat and letting the blood, drain away, 'halal', is permitted. Special prayers are said, before and after each meal, and the hand and mouth must be washed, before and after each meal.

Clothes

The Qur'an makes it clear that dress for both men and women should be modest. Today, dress for Muslims varies in different countries. Strictly speaking, Muslim women should cover their bodies, almost completely, in public. However, this does depend on the country and the convictions of the particular Muslim. It is usual to see Muslim girls in Britain, wearing shalwar (loose trousers), a kameez (a long loose top) and a veil for the head and shoulders.

Madressa (school)

Muslim children in Britain attend Qur'an classes after the normal school day.

MUSLIM FESTIVALS

Find out about the Muslim religious festivals. A few are mentioned below. The dates of the festivals vary from year to year, because the Muslim calendar is counted from the year that Muhammad went from Makkah to Medina; and they are not on the same day each year, because the Muslim months are shorter than the Christian months. Copies of the annual Calendar of Religious Festivals may be obtained from: The Shap Working Party 23, Kensington Square, London W8 5HN.

Ramadan and the Festival of Eid-ul-Fitr
Ramadan, or the month of fasting, is the ninth Islamic month. It is a very important month in the Islamic calendar. Eid-ul-Fitr takes place at the end of Ramadan. Money is given to poorer people. Special food is prepared for the feast. New clothes are bought and presents are given to each other. Special Eid cards are sent to friends (see page 96 and see Shap calendar for dates.)

Eid-ul-Adha
This is the festival that takes place at the end of Hajj or pilgrimage. If they can, each family will sacrifice a sheep or a cow, giving part of it away to families who cannot afford to make the sacrifice. This is done in remembrance of Ibrahim's willingness to sacrifice his son. (Muslims believe Ibrahim was a great prophet. You can read about this story in the Bible, Genesis, chapter 22, verses 1–19, or in the Qur'an chapter 2 verses 126–128. If the story is read in the Bible, remember that it is Isaac who is sacrificed and not Ishma'ail as stated in the Qur'an).

Muharram
This is the first month in the Muslim calendar. It is the Muslim New Year. (See Shap calendar for date.)

Melad-ul-Nabi

This is the birthday of Muhammad; the twelfth day of the third Islamic month.

Lailat-ul-Qadr

This is known as the 'Night of Power', when Muhammad received the revelations from the Angel Jibra'il. It is celebrated on the twenty-sixth night of Ramadan.

Lailat-ul-Bara'at

This is known as the 'Night of Forgiveness'. It takes place in the middle of the month *before* Ramadan in preparation for the holy month of Ramadan.

Lailat-ul-Mi'raj

This is known as the 'Night of Ascension'. It is celebrated on the twenty-sixth night of the Islamic month known as Rajab.

Resources

Books
AFDAVAN, J. *Growing Up in Islam*, Longman, 1991 (P & T).
AGGARWAL, M. *I am a Muslim*, Franklin Watts, 1984 (P).

AL-SALEH, K. *Fabled Cities, Princes and Jinn from Arab Myths and Legends*, Peter Lowe, 1985 (P & T).

BAILEY, J.R. *Religious Leaders and Places of Pilgrimage Today*, Schofield & Sims, 1987 (T).

BAILEY, J.R. *Founders, Prophets and Sacred Books*, Schofield & Sims, 1985 (T).

BAILEY, J.R. *Religious Buildings and Festivals*, Schofield & Sims, 1984 (T).

BARLOW, C. *Islam*, Batsford Academic and Educ. Ltd., 1983 (P & T).

BENNETT, O. *Festival! Ramadan and Eid Ul-Fitr*, Macmillan Educational, 1986 (P).

COLE, W.O.(Ed.) *Religion in the Multi-Faith School*, Hulton, 1983 (T).

COLE, W.O. *Five Religions in the Twentieth Century*, Hulton, 1981 (T).

COOPER, J. *Muslim Festivals*, Wayland, 1989 (P).

DROUBIE, R.E. *Islam*, Ward Lock Educ., 1973

HARRISON, S.W. and SHEPHERD, D. *A Muslim Family in Britain*, Religious and Moral Education, Press, 1980 (P & T).

HOAD, A. *Islam*, Wayland, 1986 (P).

KAMM, A. *The story of Islam*, Dinosaur Publications Ltd., 1976 (P).

PROTHEROE, R. *Visiting a Mosque*, Lutterworth Educ., 1984 (P).

ROBINSON, A. *Muhammad and The Heroes of Islam*, Schofield & Sims, 1979 (P).

THORLEY, S. *Islam in Words and Pictures*, Religious and Moral Education Press, 1982 (P & T).

TRIGGS, T.D. *Founders of Religions*, Wayland, 1981 (P).

(P) = Pupils
(T) = Teachers

Useful Addresses:

The Islamic Cultural Centre
146 Park Road
London NW8 7RG

Muslim Educational Trust
233 Seven Sisters Road
London N4

Islamic Information Services Ltd.
Trafalgar House
11 Waterloo Place
London SW1Y 4AS

Minaret House
9, Leslie Park Road,
Croydon
CR0 6TN

Pronunciation Guide to Islamic Words

Abd al–Mutt/a/lib	'Abd' as it sounds phonetically; 'al' rhymes with 'pal'; 'Mutt' as in 'moot'; long 'a'; 'lib' rhymes with 'beeb'
Ab/u Ta/lib	'Ab' as it sounds phonetically; 'u' as in 'oo'; Ta' as in 'tar'; 'lib' rhymes with 'beeb'
Ad/han	'Ad' as in 'add'; 'han' rhymes with 'fun'
Ag/ar/bat/tis	'Ag' as it sounds phonetically; 'ar' as in 'far'; 'bat' as in 'bart'; 'tis' rhymes with 'kiss'
A/lai/kum	'A' as in 'uh'; 'lai' as in 'lie'; 'kum' rhymes with 'tomb'
A/llah	'A' as in 'uh'; 'llah' long 'a' sound
A/lla/hu Ak/bar	'A' as in 'uh'; 'lla' long 'a' sound; 'hu' rhymes with 'shoe'; 'Ak' as in 'suck'; 'bar' rhymes with 'car'
Al-Mad/in/ah	'Al' rhymes with 'pal'; 'Mad' rhymes with 'sad'; 'in' as in 'been'; 'ah' as in 'car'
Al-Tash/a/hud	'Al' rhymes with 'pal'; 'Tash' as it sounds phonetically; long 'a' sound; 'hud' as in 'hood'
A/min/ah	'A' as in 'are'; 'min' rhymes with 'been'; 'ah' as in 'car'
A/qiq/a	'A' as in 'are'; 'qiq' as in 'kick'; 'a' as in 'car'
Ash had/u	'Ash' rhymes with 'dash'; 'had' as in 'hard'; 'u' as in 'shoe'
Ass/a/la/mu	'Ass' as in 'ass'; long 'a' sound; 'la' as in 'lah'; 'mu' rhymes with 'shoe'
A/than	'A' as in 'are'; 'than' rhymes with 'van'
Eid-ul-Ad/ha	'Eid' pronounced 'id'; 'ul' as in 'pull'; 'Ad' as in 'add'; 'ha' as in 'huh'
Eid-ul/Fit/r	'Eid' pronounced 'id'; 'ul' as in 'pull'; 'Fit' as in 'fit'; 'r' as in 'here'
Faj/r	'Faj' long 'a' sound; 'r' as in 'here'
Fat/i/ha	'Fat' as in 'fut'; 'i' as in 'ee'; 'ha' as in 'huh'
Hajj	'Hajj' rhymes with 'badge'
Hay/ya al/al fal/ah	'Hay' as in 'hi'; 'ya' as in 'yah'; 'al' as in 'ul'; 'fal' rhymes with 'pal'; 'ah' long 'a' sound

Hay/ya al/as sal/ah	'Hayya' as above; 'al' as in 'ul'; 'las' rhymes with 'grass'; 'sal' rhymes with 'pal'; 'ah' long 'a' sound
Hi/ra	'Hi' as in 'here'; 'ra' long 'a' sound
I/bra/him	'I' as in 'ee'; 'bra' long 'a' sound; 'him' as in 'him'
Ill/a/llah	'Ill' as in 'eel'; long 'a' sound; 'llah' long 'a' sound
I/mam	'I' as in 'ee'; 'mam' long 'a' sound
I/qua/mat	'I' as in 'ee'; 'qua' long 'a' sound; 'mat' rhymes with 'cat'
I'/sha	'I' as in 'ee'; 'sha' long 'a' sound
Jib/ra/'il	'Jib' rhymes with 'bib'; 'ra' long 'a' sound; 'il as in 'eel'
Kha/di/jah	'Kha' as in 'car'; 'di' rhymes with 'tea'; 'jah' as in 'jar'
Lai/lat ul Bar/a/'at	'Lai' as in 'lie'; 'lat' rhymes with 'cat'; 'ul' as in 'pull'; 'Bar' as in 'bar'; long 'a' sound; 'at' as in 'sat'
Lai/lat ul Mi'/raj	'Lai' as in 'lie'; 'lat' rhymes with 'cat'; 'ul' as in 'pull'; 'Mi' as in 'me'; 'raj' long 'a' sound
Lai/lat ul Qad/r	Lailat ul as above; 'Qad' as in 'quad'; 'r' as in 'here'
Mak/kah	'Mak' as in 'mack'; 'kah' as in 'car'
Me/lad-ul-Na/bi	'Me' as in 'May'; 'lad' as in 'lud'; 'ul' as in 'pull'; 'Na' long 'a' sound; 'bi' as in 'bee'
Mih/rab	'Mih' rhymes with 'here'; 'rab' long 'a' sound
Min/ar/et	'Min' rhymes with 'been'; 'ar' as in 'car'; 'et' rhymes with 'get'
Min/bar	'Min' rhymes with 'been'; 'bar' as in 'bar'
Mu/ez/zin	'Mu' rhymes with 'shoe'; 'ez' rhymes with 'fez'; 'zin' rhymes with 'bin'
Mu/har/ram	'Mu' rhymes with 'shoe'; 'har' as in 'fur'; 'ram' as in 'rum'
Qib/la	'Qib' rhymes with 'bib'; 'la' rhymes with 'car'
Qur/'an	'Qur' rhymes with 'pure'; 'an' rhymes with 'barn'
Rah/mat/u/llah	'Rah' rhymes with 'car'; 'mat' as in 'mut'; 'u' rhymes with 'shoe'; 'llah' rhymes with 'car'
Ra/ma/dan	'Ra' rhymes with 'car'; 'ma' as in 'uh'; 'dan' rhymes with 'darn'
Ras/u/llu/llah	'Ras' rhymes with 'grass'; 'u' as in 'shoe'; 'llu' as in 'shoe'; 'llah' rhymes with 'car'
Sawm	'Sawm' rhymes with 'born'
Ta/war/rok	'Ta' as in 'tar'; 'war' as in 'were'; 'rok' as in 'rock'
Wa	'Wa' rhymes with 'car'
Wud/hu	'Wud' as in 'wood'; 'hu' rhymes with 'shoe'
Zak/at	'Zak' as in 'back'; 'at' as in 'cat'
Zu/hr	'Zu' as in 'zoo'; 'hr' as in 'here'

Sikhism

Background Information

Guru Nanak

Guru Nanak was the founder of Sikhism. He was born in 1469 and died in 1539. Born into a Hindu family, situated in a Muslim village in the Punjab, Guru Nanak, spent the years after his thirtieth birthday, teaching that Hindus and Muslims were one. It was when he was thirty, that he had a vision of God, and so he began to teach the people that there was one true God, and that followers should worship Him. The words Guru Nanak spoke became known as the *Mool Mantra* or the basic Credal statement.

The Guru Granth Sahib

This is the Sikhs Holy book. It contains the writings of the Sikh Gurus. It was Guru Gobind Singh, who told the Sikhs, that there would not be another human Guru, but they should follow the sacred words of all the Gurus, that had been written down and which then became known as the Guru Granth Sahib. It was written in the Gurmurki script, and this book was, and is, treated as a living Guru.

The Ten Gurus

Listed below are the names and dates of the Ten Gurus, some of whose writings make up the Guru Granth Sahib.

Guru Nanak 1469–1539
Guru Angad 1539–1552
Guru Amar Das 1552–1574
Guru Ram Das 1574–1581
Guru Arjan 1581–1606
Guru Hargobind 1606–1644 ⎫
Guru Har Rai 1644–1661 ⎬ They did not compose
Guru Har K'ishan 1661–1664 ⎭ any hymns
Guru Teg Bahadur 1664–1675

Guru Gobind Singh 1675–1708 } His compositions are in a separate collection called the Dasam Granth.

Guru Ram Das began building the famous city of Amritsar. It was Guru Arjan who built the Golden Temple and who called it the 'House of God' or 'Har Mandir Sahib', or 'Darbar Sahib'.

Worship

This takes place in a Gurdwara (or Building) which houses the Guru Granth Sahib. The Guru Granth Sahib is usually placed on the Manji Sahib (or stool) which is situated on a raised platform called the Takht, There are no priests or ministers, the reader is called the Granthi. Sikhs will put their hands together and bow towards the Guru Granth Sahib, as a mark of respect, when entering or leaving the Gurdwara, where the Holy book is read and hymns from the Guru Granth Sahib are sung. The congregation sit crosslegged on the floor. All Sikhs whether they have been initiated into the Khalsa (or brotherhood) or not, may read from the scriptures. (see below).

SIKH FAMILY LIFE

Background Information

Naming Ceremony

Soon after the birth of a Sikh baby, 'the words of the Mool Mantra are whispered into the baby's ear and a drop of honey is placed on his or her tongue'. (Bailey: *Worship, Ceremonial and Rites of Passage.*)

Then the baby is taken to the Gurdwara to be given a name. This is chosen by randomly opening the Guru Granth Sahib, and on whichever page the book opens, the first letter of the first hymn is taken to be the first letter of the child's name.

Prayers are recited, and after the ceremony, friends and relatives join together for a celebratory meal.

The Khalsa (or Brotherhood) Initiation Ceremony

Sikhs believe that men and women are born equal and so at about the age of fourteen or fifteen, when a young Sikh is capable of being responsible for his or her own actions, he can become a full member of the Sikh Faith (or Khalsa) by taking part in the initiation ceremony called, Amrit Sanskar.

First, a young Sikh must possess the five K's of Sikhism:

Kesh — uncut hair and beard
Kangha — comb
Kaccha — shorts
Kara — steel bracelet, to be worn on the right wrist
Kirpan — sword

Then the young person must promise to obey certain rules such as; not cutting their hair or beards; not eating meat that has been prepared by a Muslim (Halal); not to commit adultery. They must promise too, to respect the words of the Guru Granth Sahib, to be honest and to give money to the poor. The young person will have learnt the words of the Mool Mantra by heart, and so will repeat these words at the ceremony. Each male Sikh is given the name Singh (meaning lion) and every girl is given the name Kaur (meaning princess).

After the ceremony Karah Prasad (food made from flour, butter, sugar etc.) is shared and eaten.

The Granthi

The Granthi or reader is trained to read from the Holy book, and he officiates at weddings and funerals. Sometimes, the Granthi also teaches the Sikh children about the Guru Granth Sahib and about the lives of the different Gurus. He may also teach the children the Gurmurki script.

Prayers and Worship

In the morning, before praying, Sikhs wash themselves, and then spend time in prayer and meditation. They will have learnt the first section of the Guru Granth Sahib called the Japji, by heart. So this can be recited, or hymns from the Gutka (also part of the Guru Granth Sahib) can be read. The prayer known as the Rehraas is said in the evening, and the prayer known as the Sohila is said before going to bed.

Weddings

The parents choose the bride or groom for their respective or son daughter. This is called an 'arranged' marriage. The wedding usually takes place in the Gurdwara with the Guru Granth Sahib. It is a very colourful affair, because the bride wears red shalwar (trousers) and kameez (tunic) and a red chunni (scarf). The father places a garland of flowers over the Guru Granth Sahib and the couple walk round the holy book four times during the service.

SIKH FESTIVALS

Baisakhi

This is the first month of the New Year in the Sikh calendar (April). Since 1699, it has become a special celebration to mark the beginning of the Khalsa or brotherhood. This is because the tenth Guru, Guru Gobind Singh, asked his followers to prove their allegiance to their Guru, by offering to die for him. Five volunteers were called for, and although the congregation heard the swish of the sword and saw blood appear outside the tent, where the volunteers were, not one was killed. They emerged, wearing new uniforms and the new brotherhood was formed (see assembly on pages 53–55).

The Birthday of Guru Nanak

The anniversary of any of the Gurus births or deaths is an occasion to hold a special celebration called a Gurpurb. Guru Nanak's birthday is celebrated in this way. There is usually a procession and the whole of the Guru Granth Sahib is read, in turn, by different readers in the Gurdwara. Afterwards there is a special feast. We know that Guru Nanak was born in 1469, and the Festival usually takes place in October/November time, although according to some scholars his actual birthday was in April.

Hola Mohalla

This Festival takes place in the Spring (March). It is very similar to the Hindu Festival, in that, bonfires are lit, and coloured water is squirted at one another, but the reason behind the Festival has a slightly different emphasis for Sikhs. It was the tenth Guru, Guru Gobind Singh, who first introduced displays of 'swordsmanship, horsemanship, archery and wrestling competitions' (J.G. Walshe, *Celebrations Across the Cultures*.)

Diwali

This winter Festival of Light (November) has special meaning for Sikhs everywhere. The sixth Guru, Guru Hargobind had been imprisoned by the Moghal Emperor, but on his release in 1620, Guru Hargobind returned to Amritsar. The Golden Temple was lit with hundreds of candles and lamps, for joy, at his return. Today, the Festival is still celebrated, and Sikhs light candles in their homes, and attend the Gurdwara for worship and festive meals.

Resources

Books

AGGARWAL, M. *I am a Sikh*. Franklin Watts, 1984 (P).

ARORA, R. *Sikhism* Wayland, 1986 (P & T).

BAILEY, J.R. *Religious Buildings and Festivals*, Schofield and Sims, 1984 (T).

BAILEY, J.R. *Founders, Prophets and Sacred Books*, Schofield and Sims, 1985 (T).

BAILEY, J.R. *Worship, Ceremonial and Rites of Passage*, Schofield and Sims, 1986 (T).

BAILEY, J.R. *Religious Leaders and Places of Pilgrimages Today*, Schofield and Sims, 1987 (T).

BAILEY, J.R. *Religious Beliefs and Moral Codes*, Schofield and Sims, 1988 (T).

CLUTTERBUCK, A. *Growing Up in Sikhism*, Longman, 1991 (P & T).

COLE, W.O. *A Sikh Family in Britain*, Religious and Moral Education Press, 1973 (P & T).

COLE, W.O. and SAMBHI, P. SINGH. *A Popular Dictionary of Sikhism*, Curzon Press Ltd., 1990 (T).

COLE, W.O. and SAMBHI, P. SINGH *Baisakhi*, Religious and Moral Education Press, 1987 (P & T).

COLE, W.O. and SAMBHI, P. SINGH *The Sikhs; their Religious Beliefs and Practices*, 1978 Routledge (T).

DAVIDSON, M. *Guru Nanak's Birthday*, Religious and Moral Education Press, 1982 (P).

GRIMMITT, M. (*et al.*), *A Gift to the Child*, Simon and Schuster, 1991 (P & T).

KAPOOR, S.S. *Sikh Festivals* Wayland, 1985 (P & T).

KAPOOR, S.S. *Sikhs and Sikhism* Wayland 1982 (P & T).

LYLE, S. *Pavan is a Sikh*, A. & C. Black., 1977 (P).

SAMBHI, P. SINGH. *Sikhism*, Stanley Thomas, 1989 (T).

(P) = Pupils
(T) = Teachers

Posters Available from:

Pictorial Charts Educational Trust
27, Kirchen Road,
London,
W13 0UD.
Tel: 081–567 9206

1   *Set no. E750 Sikh Festivals*
    (The 4 charts includes the Ten Gurus; Diwali and Baisakhi; the
    birthday of the Sikh Khalsa; and symbols such as the Five K's.)
2   *Set no. E724 Holy Places*
    (includes a picture of the Golden Temple at Amritsar.)
3   *Set no. E721 Initiation Rites*
    (includes Christian, Jewish, Sikh, Buddhist.)

Tying a Turban

Source: Pavan is a Sikh, S. Lyle published by A. and C. Black, 1977. Line drawings based on
photographs by Nick Hedges.

Pronunciation Guide to Sikh Words

Ak/hand Path 'Ak' as in 'back'; 'hand' as in 'hand'; 'Path' as in 'path'

Am/rit Sans/kar 'Am' as in 'am'; 'rit' rhymes with 'fit'; 'Sans' as in 'sands'; 'kar' as in 'car'

Am/rits/ar 'Am' as in 'am'; 'rits' rhymes with 'bits'; 'ar' as in 'far'

An/and/pur 'An' as in 'an'; 'and' as in 'and'; 'pur' as in 'poor'

Bai/sak/hi 'Bai' as in 'bye'; 'sak' rhymes with 'lark'; 'hi' as in 'he'

Bal/a 'Bal' as in 'pal'; 'a' as 'ah'

Chack/ra 'Chack' rhymes with 'Jack'; 'ra' as in 'ruh'

Dar/bar Sa/hib 'Dar' rhymes with 'far'; 'bar' rhymes with 'far'; 'sa' as in 'car'; 'hib' pronounced 'heeb'

Das/am Granth 'Das' as in 'has'; 'am' as in 'am'; 'Granth' as it sounds phonetically

Da/ya Ram 'Da' as in 'die'; 'ya' as in 'yuh'; 'Ram' as in 'ram'

Dhar/am Das 'Dhar' as in 'far'; 'am' as in 'um'; 'Das' as in 'pass'

Diw/a/li 'Diw' as it sounds phonetically; 'a' as in 'far'; 'li' rhymes with 'tea'

Du/patt/a 'Du' as in 'do'; 'patt' as in 'pat'; 'a' as in 'far'

Granth/i 'Granth' as it sounds phonetically; 'i' as in 'ee'

Gurd/war/a 'Gurd' rhymes with 'curd'; 'war' as in 'were'; 'a' as in 'ah'

Gur/mukhi 'Gur' rhymes with 'purr'; 'mukhi' as in 'mucky'

Gur/purb 'Gur' rhymes with 'purr'; 'purb' rhymes with 'curb'

Gu/ru Am/ar Das 'Gu' rhymes with 'do'; 'ru' rhymes with 'do'; 'Am' as in 'am'; 'ar' as in 'far'; 'Das' as in 'pass'

Gu/ru An/gad Guru as above; 'An' as in 'fan'; 'gad' rhymes with 'fad'

Gu/ru Ar/jan Guru as above; 'Ar' as in 'far'; 'jan' rhymes with 'fan'

Gu/ru Go/bind Rai Guru as above; 'Go' as in 'go'; 'bind' as in 'bin' plus a 'd'; 'Rai' as in 'rye'

Gu/ru Go/bind Singh Guru Gobind as above; 'Singh' as in 'sing'

Gu/ru Granth Sa/hib Guru as above; Granth as it sounds phonetically; 'sa' as in 'car'; 'hib' as in 'heeb'

Gu/ru Har/go/bind Guru as above; 'Har' as in 'car'; 'go' as in 'go'; 'bind' as in 'bin' plus a 'd'

Gu/ru Har K'ish/an Guru as above; 'Har' as in 'car'; 'K'ish' rhymes with 'dish'; 'an' as in 'can'

Gu/ru Har Rai	Guru as above; 'Har' as in 'car'; 'Rai' as in 'rye'
Gu/ru Nan/ak	Guru as above; 'Nan' as in 'nan'; 'ak' as in 'back'
Gu/ru Teg Ba/had/ur	Guru as above; 'Teg' rhymes with 'leg'; 'Ba' as in 'bah'; 'had' as in 'had'; 'ur' as in 'poor'
Gut/ka	'Gut' rhymes with 'foot'; 'ka' as in 'car'
Gwal/i/or	'Gwal' rhymes with 'pal'; 'i' as in 'me'; 'or' rhymes with 'poor'
Har Man/dir Sa/hib	'Har' as in 'car'; 'Man' as in 'mun'; 'dir' as in 'deer'; 'sa' rhymes with 'far'; 'hib' pronounced 'heeb'
Him/mat Rai	'Him' as in 'him'; 'mat' as in 'mat'; 'Rai' as in 'rye'
Ho/la Mo/hal/la	'Ho' rhymes with 'toe'; 'la' as in 'lah'; 'Mo' as in 'mow'; 'hal' rhymes with 'pal'; 'la' as in 'far'
Jap/ji	'Jap' rhymes with 'cap'; 'ji' as in 'jeep'
Kacch/a	'Kacch' as in 'catch'; 'a' as in 'far'
Kam/eez	'Kam' rhymes with 'lamb'; 'eez' as in 'breeze'
Kang/a	'Kang' as it sounds phonetically; 'a' as in 'far'
Kar/a	'Kar' as in 'car'; 'a' as in 'uh'
Kar/a Pra/sad	'Kar' as in 'car'; 'a' as in 'uh'; 'Pra' as in 'far'; 'sad' as in 'sud'
Kaur	'Kaur' rhymes with 'pour'
Kesh	'Kesh' rhymes with 'race'
Khal/sa	'Khal' rhymes with 'pal'; 'sa' as in 'far'
Khan/da	'Khand' rhymes with 'hand'; 'da' as in 'far'
Kir/pan	'Kir' rhymes with 'purr'; 'pan' as in 'pan'
Man/ji Sa/hib	'Man' as in 'man'; 'ji' as in 'jeep'; 'Sa' as in 'car'; 'hib' pronounced 'heeb'
Meht/a Ka/lu	'Meht' as in 'met'; 'a' as in 'uh'; 'Ka' as in 'car'; 'lu' rhymes with 'shoe'
Mool Man/tra	'Mool' rhymes with 'pool'; 'man' as in 'man'; 'tra' rhymes with 'far'
Muk/ham Chand	'Muk' as in 'muck'; 'ham' as in 'hum'; 'Chand' rhymes with 'hand'
Nis/an Sa/hib	'Nis' rhymes with 'kiss'; 'han' as in 'hun'; 'Sa' as in 'car'; 'hib' pronounced 'heeb'
Pal/ki	'Pal' as in 'pal'; 'ki' as in 'key'
Reh/raas	'Reh' rhymes with 'tea'; 'raas' rhymes with 'grass'
Sa/hib Chand	'Sa' as in 'car'; 'hib' pronounced 'heeb'; 'Chand' rhymes with 'hand'
Shab/ads	'Shab' rhymes with 'drab'; 'ads' as in 'adds'
So/hil/a	'So' as in 'so'; 'hil' as in 'heel'; 'a' as in 'uh'